Japanese
OBJETS D'ART

Japanese
OBJETS D'ART

By F. A. TURK

Revised & Adapted
by Judith Cohen

STERLING PUBLISHING CO., Inc.
New York

STERLING COLLECTORS SERIES

COINS THROUGH THE AGES
GUNS THROUGH THE AGES

In memoriam
DR FRANZ WEBER
(Vienna)
Obiit 10 March 1961

American edition Copyright © 1963
© FRANK A. TURK 1962

Published by Sterling Publishing Co., Inc.
419 Fourth Avenue, New York 16, New York
Manufactured in the United States of America
Library of Congress Catalog Card No.: 63–11584

Contents

Foreword

THE purposes of this small book are simple: to sketch the background of the art of Japan so that the collector and general student may come to understand its values from the viewpoints of the Japanese themselves; to provide a very short account of the historical development of styles; to give a general account of the arts so that both the processes and the necessary technical terms can be understood and to guide the reader to sources from which he may obtain further and more detailed information on the subject of each section. These book lists are headed "Further Reading"—they are just that and not necessarily to be thought of as sources, nor as validating the subject matter of the present work. Naturally, there is little original material in such a work as this, but it is hoped that it will provide a handy reference to the arts of Japan both in the library and the salesroom.

Within the limits of this book it has not been possible to touch on the subject matter of Japanese art at any greater length than to give the barest survey of the main sources solely for the purposes of the beginner. The appendices, although very brief, are an integral and important part of the work and should be of frequent use in a pocket text of this kind.

I most gratefully acknowledge the assistance I have received from Mr. Kay Larsen for photographs on plates 1 to 7, to Mr. Cyril Staal for the Satsuma bowl on plate 7, and to Miss R. Murphy for those on plate 8. Mr. Norman Hall, A.R.C.A., kindly made for me the drawings for the line blocks of the figures of Buddhas. Mr. H. L. Douch, curator of the museum of the Royal Institution of Cornwall, allowed on behalf of that body the reproduction of the articles on plates 1 to 7, and has always given much kind assistance to my studies.

Native sources have been consulted in writing this book, but have not been cited in the lists of further reading as it was thought that they would not usually be accessible to those for whom the work is primarily designed.

F. A. TURK

August 1961

Introduction

ALTHOUGH there are many difficulties inherent in the subject, the student of Japanese art has little to fear and can be certain that his efforts will be rewarded by completely new aesthetic experiences and intellectual pleasures. For the collector of Japanese art the rewards are the same—but there are traps. He may find that his enthusiasm for a work is, by Japanese standards, misdirected: he has admired it for the wrong reasons. Also he will probably discover that most of the objects he supposed to be prized works of eighteenth century masters were actually made by good craftsmen of the nineteenth or twentieth. He will probably find also that some pieces which he supposed to be Japanese perversely turn Chinese later, although he may be consoled by the thought that the reverse is even more likely to occur. To reduce these hazards; to give the student confidence by providing a guide to his studies; to indicate to him the means by which to obtain a humane authority that will allow him to forgive himself and others the blunders of inexperience: these are the aims of this handbook.

To avoid the first of these traps, the student is advised to read most carefully the section of this book which deals with Japanese aesthetic theory and to relate it to translations of Japanese poetry. With this background he should then look at as many early works of art or good reproductions as he can find. If in addition he uses the books listed in the bibliography to enlarge his knowledge, he will eventually acquire a degree of competence in evaluating Japanese art, and consequent assurance as a collector. He must also gain a knowledge of the evolution of style in each century and become familiar with the materials used (many of which are seldom met with in Western art) and how they are worked. This book sketches in the outline of such studies and should prove useful not only as a guide, but later as a resumé.

There are two ways of writing such a manual. One may, as this book does in part, treat the classes of objects, or the materials of which they are made, by means of a technological classification; or one may treat all the pure and applied arts of a single historical period together. In some ways the latter method better illustrates the social background of each period, but the former is more convenient for the collector and connoisseur, since it enables him to trace the development of style and technique in one material and so more easily put a piece in its proper setting in place and time, a principal aim of many collectors.

To avoid confusing Japanese and Chinese art it is necessary to consider briefly the characteristics of the former. Since it borrowed heavily and continuously from the Chinese it is natural to find many similarities in motifs, style, and sometimes technique, but since everything borrowed was sooner or later developed in accordance with Japanese taste, it is usually no more difficult to distinguish between Chinese and Japanese art, once both have become familiar, than it is to separate Greek and Roman. Chinese art shows a marked predilection for the highly abstract, the idealistic, and the generalized. Carved or engraved works frequently have flattened or gently curved surfaces; the plan of many is more or less oval. Japanese art is most often realistic and even naturalistic; its tendency has always been to take the generalized conceptions of Chinese art and to render them in strongly individualistic forms, often of great power even in tiny *netsuke* carvings, and fully in the round. More than the Chinese, the Japanese ignore classical Western ideas of symmetry and strive for a dynamic balance. Add a pursuit of variety which uses the most ingenious means to avoid repetition of any part of a design and a usually impeccable taste in placing the parts in relation to the whole, and one has an outline of the essential characteristics of Japanese art. One might add also that Japanese artists often show a great disregard for the limitations of their material and so are frequently able to surprise us most delightfully. They may also, however, on occasion, torture the nature of the material by too much ingenuity. This is especially true in later periods.

Amida Buddha making the mudra of *jō-in* (the gesture of the wrapt contemplation of a single object of meditation).

PART ONE

The background of Japanese art

THE great interest in Japanese art and handicrafts in recent years indicates how widespread and spontaneous the response to an exotic culture can be; however, to understand art so different from that of the West one should, ideally, study its background as thoroughly as possible. A book such as this can, obviously, no more provide a complete cultural history of Japan than it can explore in detail all the forms of Japanese art, but it may at least serve as a guide and, it is hoped, inspire further reading.

The principal sources of Japanese art are Buddhism, Shintō, Chinese art, and, less important than these, contact with the West. All had varying effects on the distinct (though not always easily distinguishable) artistic traditions of the nobility, the middle classes, and the peasantry.

SHINTŌ

Shintō is the earliest, but far from the most pervasive influence in Japanese art. The word Shintō is the Sino-Japanese reading of two ideograms that in pure Japanese read *Kami no michi*, or The Way of the Gods, and refers to the ritual surrounding the worship of the native deities. It is essentially a religion of gratitude for the wonder and beauty of everything that exists, and the worship of a pantheon of which the principal deity is the sun-goddess Amaterasu. Ritual purity is the basic obligation of Shintō, and purification ceremonies, as well as temples and shrines, are occasionally depicted in art. Shintō is a rather broad term which includes the primitive religion of Japan, whose deities and practices are sometimes found as art motifs; the thirteen or so contemporary sects; Kokutai Shintō, the worship of the Emperor as of divine origin and representing the Absolute; the imperial family's Shintō based on four shrines; and household Shintō, which centers around the family altar (*kamidana* or "god shelf"), and sometimes a small garden shrine. Small twigs of the *sakaki* tree and *gohei*, cuttings made from folded paper and

(Left) *Gohei* of cut and folded papers on a stick. (Right) *Tamagushi* offering to a Shinto god: a sprig of the sacred *Sakaki* tree (*Eurya ochnacea*).

attached in rows to a wand, are important in household Shintō and appear very often as decorative motifs.

Most important of all is Shrine Shintō. There are said to be some 110,000 shrines in Japan and their architecture, like their ritual, shows Buddhist and sometimes Taoist influence. The Grand Shrine of Ise with its fourteen subsidiaries is the greatest; the buildings and rituals are sometimes shown in prints and books. The wooden shrine buildings consist usually of the sanctuary (*honden*) and the hall of worship (*haiden*), which are approached by the familiar two-pillar gateway or *torii*. Shintō buildings can usually be told from Buddhist by the horn-like finials on the roof which keep the ridge beam in place; Shintō finials are somewhat scissors-shaped and are called *chigi*. In the shrines are kept the *shintai* (God body), which include such objects as swords, mirrors, stones, in which reside the *mitama* (august jewels)—the spirits or doubles of the gods.

The pantheism of Shintō embodies the all-pervading love of natural objects, even the most insignificant, so characteristic of Japanese art. The fifteenth-century poet Urabe-no-Kanekuni expresses the essence of Shintō as

> Manifesting Itself
> Is the awe-evoking Deity
> Even in a single leaf
> Or the weakest grass blade.

A key to this attitude is given in the fourteenth-century diary of Saka Jubutsu as translated by Genchi Katō in his book *What is Shintō?*: "Washing oneself in the sea-water and being cleansed of bodily filth—this is outer purity. Being pure in mind and body, our soul is united with the Divine and, divinity in humanity thus realized, there remains no desire unsatisfied—there is no occasion for further petition to the Goddess. This is the true esoteric meaning of worshipping the Goddess at the Ise Shrine. Being thus enlightened by the priest of the shrine, I was overwhelmed with a sense of pious joy and burst into tears of gratitude."

Further Reading

Genchi Katō, Dr, *What is Shintō?* Tourist Library No. 8, Tōkyō, 1935.

Aston, W. G., *Shintō: the Ancient Religion of Japan*, London, 1907.

Abe Kuniharu, 'The Essence of Shrine Shintō', *Trans. Meiji Japan. Soc.*, vol. 40, pp. 56–7, Tōkyō, Sept. 1933.

Abe Kuniharu, 'A Chat on Japanese Votive Pictures', *The Tourist*, pp. 45–8, Tōkyō, July 1924.

Akiyama Aisaburo, *Shintō and its Architecture*, Tōkyō, 1937.

Holtom, D. C., 'Japanese Votive Pictures—the Ikoma Ema', *Monumenta Nipponica*, vol. 1, pp. 154–64, Tōkyō, 1938.

Fujishima Gaijiro, 'Torii and its significance', *Contemporary Japan 1942*, pp. 1–18.

Satow, E. M., 'The Shintō Temples of Ise', *Trans. Asiatic Soc. Japan*, vol. 2, pp. 99–121.

BUDDHIST

Buddhism has been by far the major force in the shaping of Japanese culture. Coming to Japan by way of India, Korea, and China, it brought with it also from those great civilizations many customs and arts unconnected with religion.

Buddhism first appeared in Japan in A.D. 552, when the King of Kudara in Korea sent to the Emperor Kinmei a bronze image of Sakyamuni Buddha, together with some Buddhist writings and ritual implements. It received great impetus in the seventh century when prince Shōtoku Taishi ordered many temples, including the famous Hōryuji, to be built at Nara. The prince also wrote commentaries

13

(Left) *Jizo* (the Bodhisattva *Ksitigarbha*) who normally holds a sistrum (*shakujō*) symbolizing his benevolence. (Right) *Kannon* (Chinese *Kuan-yin*) with lotus and vase, two of the attributes often found with this form of the goddess identified as *Ekadasamukha* (Sanskrit).

on three of the most important sutras, and these served as the foundation of Buddhist doctrine in the early days of its acceptance in Japan. Together with a few other sutras which were introduced later, these were the basis of Buddhist teaching in the Nara period (710-784), which left its mark on Japanese art, aesthetics and literature for centuries. It is remarkable that these rare philosophical doctrines should have appealed equally to scholarship and to intuition, and in them is to be found the source of most of the artistic impulses of the Japanese for the next thousand years.

Buddhism in Japan derived solely from the Mahayana (Great Raft) school, which had already moved a long way from the simplicity of the teachings of Buddha, as well as from the form of Buddhism known as Hinayana, or Little Raft. In Japan itself Buddhism divided into many schools, which differed greatly in interpretation and ritual. In considering the world as it is, or seems to be, the early schools diverged widely in their ideas of what constituted reality; the Kusha school considered the self to be unreal and thought only such elements as sensation and memory exist; the Jō-Jitsu believed the only reality was the instantaneous present moment of perception (*setsuna*); the Sanron school went still further in denying reality, but it was this school which inspired much of the

(Left) *Nyōirin Kannon* (*Cintamani-çakra*) the esoteric six-armed form of Kannon, goddess of mercy. (Right) *Dainichi Nyōrai* (the Buddha *Vairocana*) making the mudra of the *Chi ken-in*, a gesture variously interpreted as symbolic of the knowledge which will conduct souls to Paradise, or of the power of suppressing spiritual darkness, or expressive of the vast and ineffable omniscience of *Vairocana*.

15

(Left) *Monju* (*Manjusri; Samantabhadra*). (Right) *Shakamuni*, the historical buddha making the mudra of *segan-semui-in* (the gesture of the giving of fearlessness).

art and culture of the country. Sanron had its center in the sanctuary of Hōryuji, whose *kura,* or treasure house, contains many examples of Japan's most noble and most ancient art, works which should be studied by anyone wanting to understand the Japanese approach to aesthetics.

The Hossō sect, less under Hindu influence than those already mentioned, taught that thought alone was real. The highly mystical Kegon school practiced the meditation of the infinite myriads of Buddha-worlds, each reflecting the others, in every grain of dust. The Tendai took this teaching further and related it to the universal Buddhist moral law of kindness based on the belief that all things share a common Buddhahood and all move towards its fulfillment. The ornately ritualistic Shingon sect held that the essence of the universe is the Great Illuminator (Mahavairocana-Buddha); he appears in two aspects, an exoteric and an esoteric, and the Shingon follower devotes himself to sharing in the latter. Shingon has produced much of the great religious art of Japan: the mystical diagrams (*mandala*); the great scroll paintings of the many Buddhas, each emanations and reflections of one another, which are hung above the dead and welcome the soul into bliss; the innumerable statues of Buddhist divinities; lacquered boxes for sutras, decorated with scenes and designs; boxes for priests' robes; bronze ewers; and many other articles evolved for its elaborate rituals, all contributing to produce some of the world's greatest religious art.

In the following centuries political upheavals, culminating in civil war, gave rise to different approaches to religion. One way led to the simpler belief that one need only call on the Amida Buddha in complete trust to be led to the peace and beauty of the Western Paradise. The other way led to the world-forsaking discipline of Zen, the search for *satori*, an untranslatable term referring to the individual moment of enlightenment. (The classic example is Buddha's Flower Sermon. Buddha, standing among his disciples, did not speak, but held up a golden lotus. Only one of his followers, Mahakasyapa, understood. He smiled, and Buddha appointed him as his successor.) The first way gave up the struggle for enlightenment to rely instead on the saving grace of the Boddhisatva; Zen allowed the intuitional mind, in one long-planned-for instant, to encompass the truth.

Zen was considerably influenced by the old Chinese philosophy of Tao. Both Tao and Zen, and the art to which the latter gave rise (the rapid *sumiye* black ink sketch on rough paper) practiced the value of emptiness, the space in which the spirit might be set free. Equally valued in art, as in fencing and archery, which Zen also influenced, was effortlessness, so that the highest attainment in many art products is the appearance of artlessness, which may be understood as the thing in its own state of innerliness, or its own greatest self-realization.

Some understanding of Buddhist belief is essential for an understanding of Japanese art, and reading in this field will prove highly rewarding in terms of rich insights, of the building of an informed taste, and in the appreciation of references which would otherwise be lost. In this religious art many materials and techniques were brought to an early perfection. This is particularly true of architecture and later of gardening, but it is almost equally so for sculpture. As early as the Tempyō period (710-794) Japanese sculptors were creating works in the dried lacquer technique (*Kuanshitsu*), casting great statues in bronze, molding whole groups, like the Twelve Guardian Kings of the Shin Yakushiji at Nara, in clay, carving a series of famous Kwannons in wood, bringing the art of the mask to high perfection; and creating a superbly realistic portraiture statuary like that of the priest Ganjin in the Tōshōdaiji, in *papier mâché*. The religious painting of the earlier periods—the paradise of Amida, the Amida of the mountains, the Nachi Waterfall attributed to the almost legendary Kose no Kanaoka, all bear witness to one of the great peaks of religious art. Once the early fervor had ebbed, such heights were never to be reached again.

(Left) Yamagoshi-no-Amida making the mudra of the *an-i-in* (the gesture of welcoming into Paradise). (Right) *Fudo Myō-ō* (*Acalanatha*) with his commonest attributes, the sword and lasso.

Further Reading

Anesaki, M., *Buddhist Art*, Cambridge, U.S.A., 1915.

Bukkyō Bijutsu Shiryō (Collection of Illustrations of Buddhist Art), Tōkyō, 1923.

Hōryuji Taikō, Tōkyō, 1916, et seq. (Treasures at Hōryuji, Nara.)

Ōnō Gemmyō, *Daijō Bukkyō Gei jutsushi no Kenkyu* (Studies in Mahayana Buddhist Art), Tōkyō, 1929.

Pier, G. C., *Temple Treasures of Japan*, New York, 1914.

Cram, R. A., *Impressions of Japanese Architecture*, London, 1931.

Sawa Ryuken, *Mikkyō Bijutsu Ron* (On the Arts of Esoteric Buddhism), Benrido, Kyōto, 1955. (With many fine illustrations and diagrams and the most accessible of the works that deal with this abstruse subject.)

Suzuki, D. T., 'Buddhist, especially Zen contributions to Japanese Culture', *The Eastern Buddhist*, vol. 6, No. 2, pp. 111–38, June, 1933.

Grousset, R., *In the Footsteps of the Buddha*, London, 1932. (An extremely readable account of the development of the Mahayana and essential reading for acquiring a well-founded background to this art.)

'Exhibition of Japanese Buddhist Arts', Tōkyō National Museum, Tōkyō, 1956. (The most easily accessible and cheapest source of reproductions of some of the best of Japanese Buddhist art of all kinds.)

Reischauer, A. K., *Studies in Japanese Buddhism*, New York, 1925.

Eliot, Sir C., *Japanese Buddhism*, London, 1935. (A classic statement of the theme.)

Suzuki, D. T., *Japanese Buddhism*, Tourist Library, Tōkyō, 1938.

Suzuki, D. T., *Manual of Zen Buddhism*, London, 1950. (Besides much most excellent material it contains illustrations of some common themes in Buddhist art, such as the Ten Oxherding Pictures.)

Tokuzo Sagara, Prof., *Japanese Fine Arts*, Japan Travel Bureau, 1949. (Chaps. 8 and 9 of this work give an excellent short account of Buddhist art.)

19

Griessmaier, V., *Zenga—Malerei des Zen-Buddhismus in Japan Sonderausstellung*, Österreichisches Museum für Angewandte Kunst, Vienna, 1959.

Saunders, E. D., *Mudrā*, London, 1960. (Prof. Saunders's erudite and scholarly work is an essential preliminary study to any real understanding of Japanese Buddhist iconography. It is however difficult to correlate its terms with the Sanskrit ones normally used.)

CHINESE

Japanese culture, as is generally known, owed very much indeed to the older and more mellow culture of China. Its system of writing was solely Chinese in origin—a system originally evolved for a monosyllabic language but adapted, although with great and lasting difficulty, to polysyllabic Japanese. Even the Japanese attitude to imperial rule seems to owe much to Chinese and Confucian sources.

Prince Shōtoku Taishi established relations with the Sui dynasty of China (A.D. 589-619), at the peak of its luxury and power, in 607. The first mission to the T'ang court, in 630, put Japan directly in touch with that great artistic period; in 806 the priest Kukai (Kōbō Daishi) returned from China with new Buddhist doctrines, and from then on, with occasional intermissions, there was continual contact with China. So highly was Chinese influence prized, and so deeply did it penetrate into the national life, that such an abstruse matter as the Chinese Yin-Yang theories of cosmology had a special department of the government devoted to it. It is not surprising therefore that the arts show this influence to such a great extent. In even minor works it is to be seen in subject matter; such arts as *netsuke* portray characters from Chinese legends, such as Taoist immortals (*sennin*), fabulous animals, etc. This is especially true of *netsuke* made after the time of the fifth Tokugawa Shōgun, Tsunayoshi, who made the ethics of the Chu Hsi school of Confucianism the official orthodoxy. The influence went still deeper than this, and after Eisei returned from China in 1191, bringing tea and founding the Zen sect, Japan took over Chinese styles and aspirations more completely than ever.

In some arts the styles lasted more or less unchanged for centuries, as in ceramics, where Chinese forms predominated although usually modified by the coarser materials available at most kilns, until, in the seventeenth century, when such men as Ninsei were active, Japanese genius finally asserted itself.

The aspirations of the Chinese artists were, however, usually quickly modified. As an example, the wonderful portrait art of the Chinese Sung Dynasty, developed by the Ch'an (Zen) sect, was intended to exhibit in the human face and form the super-cosmic principle which was sought in Zen meditation; in a short while the Japanese artists subtly changed this to an art of intense individuality: this is the priest just as he looked in old age, but his deep spiritual experience is also made manifest; beyond all this is a suggestion of that ineffable reality that was the inspiration for the Chinese proto-type of the portrait. Such an example is repeated, on a smaller scale, in most of the arts, but the copies seem to become more automatic, less transformed, after 1339, the year in which a very active trade relation was opened between the two countries. In the following century the great painter Sesshu spent six years in China and was highly honored at the Ming court. The Japanese point of view as-serted itself in his work, however, and in all his paintings—landscape, birds and flowers, portraits—it is the individual aspect rather than the universal, that is portrayed.

Further Reading
'Chinese Art Objects introduced into Japan in the Ashikaga Period', *Kokka*, vol. 25, 1914–15, No. 301.
Grosse, E., 'Chinesische Kunstwerke in Japan und China', *Ostasiatische Zeitsch*, vol. 4, 1915–16, pp. 88–108.
Yokoi, T., 'Japan and China, their similarities and dissimi-larities', *Trans. Proc. Japan Soc.*, vol. 15, 1916–17, pp. 134–46, London.

In 1542 Mendez Pinto, a Portuguese, landed in Japan, and seven years later Saint Francis Xavier, with many priests, landed in Satsuma. Before 1600 there were said to be over a million converts to Christianity. In 1578 a Japanese embassy toured Europe and brought back many examples of religious art which were to have a lasting, though diminishing, effect. Contact ended in 1637 when Christianity was outlawed, but a tenuous relation with the West persisted, since the Dutch were allowed to continue trading from the tiny island of Deshima at Nagasaki. Their presence made possible the rise of a very small but highly significant group of notable Japanese savants who studied intensively the new arts and sciences from Europe. Short as the Portuguese contact was, it also left its mark. Portuguese merchants introduced tobacco, clocks, hats, eyeglasses, trousers, and chairs, and several Portuguese words entered the language [e.g. *raxa* (Port.)=*rasa* (Jap.) woolen cloth].

The Portuguese effect on art, however, is not easy to find, probably because so much was destroyed when Christianity was outlawed. We can see the Portuguese at work and play in some twenty pairs of screens of the kind called *namban* (lit. southern barbarian), painted by the school of Kanō painters, and showing the foreigners with their ladies, shops, animals, priests, weapons, etc. Other genre paintings of this kind are known, one of which shows the inside of a Christian church. Other arts show the same influence: a Satsuma porcelain figure of Christ, several early carved ivories depicting Christ carrying the Cross, the Madonna and Christ, and Adam and Eve are known. There are also several small silver water bottles with European letters on them which were perhaps intended to carry holy water. Similar bottles were made later for the Dutch, as were lacquer boxes with similar initials and in one case the date (1822) and a Dutch name. There are also *inrō* which show the Portuguese themselves; Japanese designs using cupids and other Western classical motifs; and one of the illustrations in the earliest Japanese work on *netsuke*, the *Shoken Kisho* (1786), was copied from a Spanish design for embossed leather.

Dutch influence was steadier and has persisted in many native works of art. Through the Dutch such artists as Shiba Kōkan learned to use European perspective (such pictures were called *Uki-e*, or bird's-eye pictures) and prints of Toyoharu's show this technique. Copperplate engraving was done, but early work of this kind is rare. The *Nagasaki-e* color prints showed many aspects of the life of the Dutch on Deshima, their shipping, and their annual journey to Yedo carrying gifts and, probably more important, information to the court of the Shōgun. Dutchmen, often carrying trumpets or cockerels, are frequently found as *netsuke* figures, as are *netsuke* in the shape of some of the Western inventions introduced by the Dutch, such as firearms and telescopes. There are also Western-style oil paintings by eighteenth century Japanese artists, their subjects usually being portraits of Westerners or of foreign shipping. The painters are for the most part members of the Araki and Ishizaki schools.

Another class of pictures was done under Dutch influence: the *doro-e* (mud pictures) carried out in a mixture of water colors and chalk. The most important of the Dutch influences was their effect on the work of Maruyama Ōkyo (1733-95), founder of the Shijō or naturalistic school of Japanese painting, who painted in oils using Western perspective. The applied arts also showed Dutch influence, at least in their choice of themes, such as Western shipping. Some Imari porcelain uses these motifs and a large amount of the early Hizen ware imported into Europe was made to the special order of the Dutch; this kind of porcelain has overladen ornamentation, mostly of flowers, quite unlike native taste.

Further Reading

Tressan, Marquis de, 'Influences étrangères dans la formation de l'art japonais', *Ann. du Mus. Guimet, Bibl. de Vulg.*, vol. 40, Paris, 1914.

Boxer, C. R., *Jan Compagnie in Japan 1600–1800*, The Hague, 1950.

Keene, D., *The Japanese Discovery of Europe*, London, 1952.

Huish, M. B., 'The Influence of Europe on the Art of Old Japan', *Trans. Japan Soc.*, vol. 2, pp. 77–110, London.

Nagami, T., *Namban Byobu Kogeisha*, Tōkyō, 1930.

Mendonça, Jose Maria de, 'Portugal in India, China and Japan', *Oriental Art*, Summer 1956, pp. 60–3.

Gray, Basil, 'Western Influence in Japan', *Oriental Art,*
Winter 1956, pp. 129–37.
Boxer, C. R., *The Christian Century in Japan 1549–1650,*
Cambridge, 1951.
Volker, T., *Porcelain and the Dutch East India Company,*
Leiden, 1954.

The Three Traditions

It is essential to realize the existence of three different traditions in Japanese art; although they often cannot be separated each has had a strong influence. To ignore them is to court confusion in understanding the different kinds of taste that are easily discernible below the surface of the art of the country.

The taste shown in folk art is much like that to be found in peasant art everywhere: very bright but harmonious colors, traditional designs varying considerably from region to region, and a spontaneous air of childlike pleasure. These qualities are found in objects which are used as implements of everyday life, such as toys, in adjuncts of peasant dress, or for ritualistic purposes in divination and exorcism. Japanese toys are to be found almost everywhere and are an aspect of the country's art which has not yet received the serious study it deserves. Other facets of folk taste are to be seen in such crafts as basketwork and the smaller articles of furniture in country farmhouses, which almost always have a feeling of ingenious and well-tried design, and in the plates with underglaze designs which were placed under the old drip lamps. These last are perhaps the most appealing to Western tastes.

The aristocratic tradition manifested itself in art from very early times and was cultivated by a small circle of hereditary nobles (*daimyō*) and later by their armed retainers (*samurai*). This aristocracy was a native one and did not represent, at least in historic times, a conquering race; its traditions and tastes were early formed and more or less strictly adhered to. Extreme sensitivity in anything pertaining to one's honor, utter loyalty, and absolute self-control were the primary virtues of the *samurai* and of their code of Bushidō;

A Seal box. Inside: *fundame nashiji-nuri*: handle in early style *Shippō* enamels. Decor of the seal boxes in *heidatsu* with a design of chrysanthemums. Exterior: *rō-iro nuri* with a decoration of vine over an ornamental *Bugaku* curtain in *takamaki-ye*. The six small drum-like containers stand in sockets. Height 1⅜ inches, length 3⅞ inches, width 2⅜ inches.

courage, courtesy, a sense of justice, and ready sympathy were the result of adherence to these qualities. If we add that calligraphy was an important subject in the education of these men, we find it natural that their art is one of understatement and of an essential reticence. The abstruse though rich nature of its associations caused it to be cultivated by a rather small group, its charms being too recondite and its taste too austere for those of different backgrounds. Yet even within this tradition there seems to have been an undercurrent of desire for the more resplendent and ornate which repeatedly showed itself in such works as the gorgeous screen paintings of the splendid Momoyama palaces or the elaborate Tokugawa tombs at Nikkō. Even in these, however, all is controlled by the same good taste. Typical of the interests and tastes of this class are the theatre of the Nō, the ink sketch, and the arts of the sword.

Equally typical of bourgeois taste are the color print, painted porcelains, and the theatre of the Kabuki—more colorful, more frivolous, with a grosser appeal to the senses, full of action and ornament and with a malicious wit and love of scandal taking the place of the obscure and mist-wreathed suggestion of the aristocrat. This tradition is no older than the seventeenth century, when political, economic, and social changes, together with improved scientific techniques in agriculture and industry immeasurably improved the lot of the townsfolk, the traders, and the artisan classes (*chōnin*), and a middle class society arose.

Although in later art the traditions of the three groups often intermingle, the student will obtain a more sensitive and accurate understanding of Japanese art if he is always aware of them in all their manifestations.

Further Reading
Nitobe, I., *Bushido; the Soul of Japan*, London and Tōkyō, 1899.
Okakura, Y., *The Japanese Spirit*, London, 1905.
Binyon, L., *Painting in the Far East*, 4th ed. rev., London, 1934. (Chapters vii and viii, and xiii to xvii are germane.)
Munsterberg, H., *The Folk Arts of Japan*, Rutland, Vermont, 1959.

THE INFLUENCE OF THOUGHT AND LANGUAGE ON ART

Anthropologists tell us that the modes of men's thought and even their experience are conditioned in large part by their language. Japanese differs not only from all European languages but also from most other Asiatic tongues. Sir George Sansom, in his *Historical Grammar of Japanese*, says, "The Indo-European languages have formal grammatical categories corresponding to certain psychological categories—word classes, such as nouns corresponding to the psychological category 'thing' . . . In Japanese either the psychological category is not fully differentiated or the correspondence between grammatical and psychological categories is incomplete." Nouns, for instance, have neither number or gender and are, in fact, universal, rather than particular. Abstract nouns, except for those taken from the Chinese, are expressed by the use of a verb or adjective, plus the word "*koto*"—thing. Any part of a sentence which describes a state of affairs or a quality can be used as if it were a noun. As a result, a philosophic subject, a poetic feeling about a landscape, or an action which to Westerners would be a matter of vague emotion can, to the Japanese, immediately take on substance. Therefore, such things are not to be considered quite in the way we consider symbols in the West. Another rule of Japanese syntax is that qualifying words or clauses precede the thing qualified, while a vast number of particles put after the word allow for refinements of classification that go far beyond what is possible in English. All of this allows for differentiations in the process of substantiation that must be experienced to be appreciated. Yet there is a simplicity and directness about the expression of thought that is proved by the possibility of leaving out words in Japanese that to us would seem to be vital to the meaning of a sentence. Parallel to this are the empty spaces, the areas of the design covered with "mist haze" or a rain of gold flakes, all perfectly natural to a people whose language leaps from noun to noun and blends dissimilar aspects into an immediate and coordinate harmony.

There is another aspect of the language which should be pointed out: since there are only forty-seven sounds in Japanese for the pronunciation of many thousands of words it is obvious that there must be thousands of homophones and partial homophones; this makes possible not only countless puns—a serious device in literature for playing on the overtones of words—but also allows words or pictures to suggest others which are quite unrelated in their meaning. To quote an example given by Dr. Donald Keene: "The word *shiranami*, meaning white waves or the wake behind a boat, might suggest to a Japanese the word *shiranu*, meaning unknown, or *namida*, meaning tears. Thus we have blending into one another three ideas: unknown, white waves, tears. One can easily see how from such a combination of such images a poem could grow . . ." and, in the same way, a picture. So a design or a sculpture may represent things other than itself by the evocation of meanings and images evolved from the puns that would come naturally to mind: a painting of wind blowing through autumn maples may evoke ideas of nostalgia or heartsick desire since *kogarashi* may mean both "autumn wind" and "to yearn for." Thus some works of art, although only a minority, communicate, intentionally, on more than one level of meaning at the same time.

Further Reading
Keene, D., *Japanese Literature; an introduction for western readers*, London, 1953.

THE VOCABULARY OF JAPANESE AESTHETICS

A study of the terms used by Japanese writers on aesthetics offers the easiest path to understanding the attitude of the Japanese toward their own art. The vocabulary of the arts indicates clearly the categories of emotional and aesthetic experience to which the Japanese are most responsive and the qualities they find most admirable. The following are short notes on terms conveying the chief experiences cherished by Japanese art lovers.

AWARE. Originally an exclamation of surprise or delight, it came to mean the type of pleasure to be found in gentle melancholy. Later there was intended by the word something with more than a touch of sorrow, particularly the sadness that comes from reflecting on the evanescence of beauty. By extension it took on the vaguer connotation of anything that is found to be extremely moving— something evoked by an uprush of feelings and emotions, not all of which are necessarily in harmony, but which brings us to the brink of tears or at least of a sigh.

EN is applied to those things which Western taste would describe as exquisite. It is more a visual and superficial quality and includes even what we would term fascinating.

OKASHII (syn. *warawashi*). A term applied to anything delightfully humorous. It can be applied to the maliciously witty and also, ironically, to the tragic. Some of the subjects of color prints exemplify this and often, as with Hiroshige and others, the poems which are superscribed on them.

MIYABI. Roughly, it means elegant, refined, or polished and is applied to whatever gives a quiet, delicate pleasure. It involves the nice discrimination of values which characterizes an aristocratic taste and is the opposite of the crude, vulgar, or boorish.

MU. The original meaning of this word was nothing, voidness. It was used in a technical sense as equal to the Sanskrit *Sunyata* in Buddhist philosophy and came also to have the significance of emptiness and particularly emptied of Self, unattached to the Self, or devoid of Ego-feeling. The reverse of individuality, it shows itself in the arts as a quality which was particularly prized by those crafts which were influenced by Zen: it is the form produced by spontaneous reaction to the circumstances of the moment without planned-for effect, but a reaction conditioned by traditional ways of experience. As Bernard Leach says, "It is the quality we most admire in pots and it is that rare condition of which we catch glimpses in men and women when the Spirit of Life blows through them as wind through an open window." It is this lack of self-display which leads to *Shibusa*, a certain degree of astringency, and therefore produces a significant form unalloyed with inconsequential sweetness, or meretricious effect. This term has, in modern times, become the basic one in the philosophy of the Japanese Craft Movement.

YUGEN. This term, which literally means profound or mysterious, is the most difficult of all to define. It is applied to something that lies beyond art and which is sensed intuitively. Indeed, the word sometimes means occult. It is thought of as belonging to a realm of absolute value that lies beyond the forms of art but is that to which all forms point. It is most easily evoked by bare, sparse, very simple but not necessarily powerful forms—those which, as one critic has said, have in them "the lines of eternity." It is essentially a characteristic of the art of the medieval period and is most commonly found in the Nō plays and in the tea ceremony. Another aspect is the "eternal loneliness" or the "truth of Aloneness" which is found in the *Lankavatarasutra* which plays such an important part in Zen doctrine. It is said to appear when the world of particulars governed by space, time, and causation is left behind. It can be seen in such paintings as the late Muromachi period screen of a moonlit

A. Kusari-Ita (a pouch clasp). Silver and copper in layers and chiselled to imitate guri-bori lacquer. B. *Kozuka* handle. A design of chrysanthemum and lace wing flies engraved in copper with an inlaid design of a *higetombo* (*Ascalaphus* sp.). Signed: Tomotake (Yokoya School). Length $3\frac{7}{8}$ in., width $\frac{5}{8}$ in. C. *Kozuka*. A cuckoo (*hototogisu*) flying before a rising moon and a spray of sweet flag. *Shakudo* with *nanako* ground with inlay of silver and *shibuichi*. D. *Kusari-Ita* (a pouch clasp). *Shibuichi* finely inlaid in a pattern of diapers in lines of *shakudo*.

landscape by an anonymous painter in the National Museum at Tōkyō and it is expressed obliquely in the little poem by the famous poet Bashō (1643-94):

> Bough leaf bare;
> Crow perching there . . .
> Autumn's evening air.

SABI. Aspiration for the rarefied *Yugen* all but disappeared from later art but *Sabi* remained very much a living reality, constantly sought for and frequently achieved. It may be applied to whatever is old and imperfect—even rusted or tarnished. It is partly that kind

Enlarged detail of *togidashi zogan* inlay of D.

of appeal which collectors of old coins find in the specimen that is beautifully patinated: it suggests something quiet and a little melancholy, like the spiritual beauty of old age seen through a time-worn face. Much of the ceramics and metalwork made for the tea ceremony show this quality, and common to them all, almost without exception, is that they rigidly avoid any semblance of finish, which is the antithesis of *sabi*. The essential quality for the existence of *sabi*, like the profound beauty of old age, is *makoto*, or sincerity. It is the thing as it is, not to be refurbished with a false personality by having the dents removed or the surface burnished, or by being regilded.

SHIBUMI (adj. *shibui*). This is a term usually applied to a certain kind of color scheme or colored pattern. It implies an astringent quality and a consideration for others in that there is a complete lack of ostentation and always a certain reticence and simple good manners. It can be applied to almost anything; in the matter of color it would be mostly applied to such hues as russet, chestnut, ashes, tarnished silver, bran, or any dull low color with a certain faded luster. It cannot be applied to colorless articles like ivory *netsuke*, but might be used for certain lacquered surfaces, although a shell inlay would probably destroy it.

SEIDO. Applied particularly to painting, especially the rapid ink sketch. It refers to the inner life-movement, the essential distinctive nature of the thing to be painted which makes it what it is.

ESORAGOTO. Refers to a certain invention in a work of art which, although factually false to nature, heightens the natural effect. It is the studied violence of a photographic likeness which makes the tiger more tiger-like.

KI-IN. That which gives the essential dignity to a work of art, ennobles it and makes it, perhaps, immortal. One writer renders it "spiritual elevation."

NOTAN. The original meaning of this term is density, as of a liquid; it is applied in painting to the density of ink tone to give a feeling of light and shade. We can recognize density of line and density of mass.

SUKI. Its general meaning of artistic taste or fancy is more particularly applied to anything luxurious or elaborate or even expensive which has most markedly the character of artlessness or naturalness.

Further Reading
Bary, W. T. de, *Sources of the Japanese Tradition*, Part II, Chapter 9, and Part III, Chapter 14. New York, 1958. (Scholarly and essential reading.)

Tea Bowl (Kiōto ware). Close grained, hard, drab-colored body covered with thick *temmoku* type glaze, the reserved design filled with a clear glaze. Nineteenth century.

THE INFLUENCE OF THE CHA-NO-YU (TEA CEREMONY)

A formal tea drinking ritual was practiced by Buddhist priests in China during the Sung Dynasty: it was introduced into Japan by the priest Musō Kokushi and the accepted ritual established in 1472 by another priest, Murata Shuko, who had an influential patron in the Shōgun Yoshimasa. Eventually, exceedingly complex rules governing every action of the ceremony were evolved and long study of these made one a *Cha-no-yu-shi* or "Master" of the art. Higher still were the *Chajin*, who laid down new regulations as necessary and became the acknowledged final arbiters of taste, not only in matters of art but also in the realm of morals. For them to stigmatize an action, a judgment, or an object of art as being "Not Tea" was similar to the connotation formerly given to the British phrase, "Not Cricket."

The *Cha-shitsu* or tea-room was usually about ten feet square, with a small opening through which the guests crawled to enter; in the *tokonoma* or alcove would be exhibited a fine ink painting, a piece of calligraphy, together with an old bronze or perhaps a special flower arrangement. Here the tea was served and every one of the necessary implements for this had to conform to certain aesthetic standards and be handled in a special manner. The *cha-shitsu* was approached through a garden—the art of garden design was greatly affected by the requirements of the *Cha-no-yu*—and the various parts of the *roji* or garden path served a particular purpose; even the

33

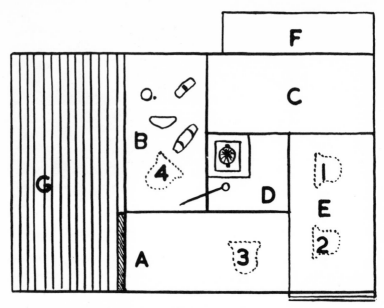

A four-and-a-half-mat tea-house (re-drawn from Okakura's *The Book of Tea*). A. Entry Mat. B. Utensil Mat. C. Distinguished Guest Mat. D. Hearth Mat. E. Guest Mat. F. *Tokonoma*. G. Utensil Room. 1. 1st or chief guest. 2. 2nd guest. 3. 3rd guest. 4. Host.

privy, with its low shingled roof, cedar-wood door, bamboo-formed window and old stone water basin was an object of cool, simple elegance and the greatest refinement of taste, teaching the truth of the inevitable changes of the body and inviting meditation on the endless vicissitudes of life.

The taste of the *Chajin* still influences the great Japanese connoisseurs; rough peasant-like ceramic wares, bowls influenced by the Sung potters of China—celadons, *temmoku* glazes in rustbrown and black—as well as the underglaze blue and white of the Ming potters, are those preferred above all others. Also simple bamboo vases for the flowers, a bamboo basket for the charcoal and old iron kettles by famous masters of the past are what are really prized. Noted types were often given nicknames like that of "Flat Spider" or "Hag's mouth" given to two historical kettles. There is, indeed, hardly an art that the *Cha-no-yu* has not affected in some way or

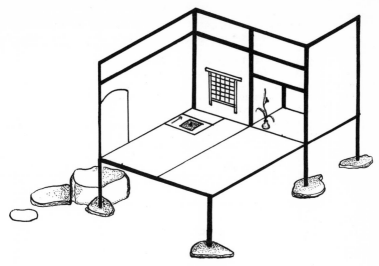

A two-mat tea-house.

other, and some knowledge of it is essential to the informed collector or general student.

Further Reading

Okakura Kakuzo, *The Book of Tea*, New York, 1906, reprint Sydney, 1935.

Fukukita Yasunosuke, *Tea Cult of Japan*, Tōkyō, 1934. (With an excellent glossary and interesting photographs.)

Jenyns, S., 'The Tea Ceremony', *Bull. Japan Soc.*, No. 33, London, Feb. 1961. 'Cha-no-yu or ceremonial Tea', *Japan Magazine*, Vol. 1, 1910–11, pp. 637–43.

Holme, C., 'The Cha-no-yu pottery of Japan', *Studio*, vol. 46, 1909–10, pp. 29–45. (With a number of good plates.)

Holme, C., 'The Pottery of the Cha-no-yu', *Trans. Proc. Japan Soc.*, vol. 8, 1909, pp. 163–86.

Anka, E., 'O Cha og Setomono', *Kunst og Kultur*, vol. 12, 1924–25, pp. 177–85. (A useful short study of pottery and the Tea Ceremony.)

B.C. 4500 to 250	**NEOLITHIC PERIOD** (dates vary in different parts of the country). Phallic worship and stone and pottery objects connected with it found. 660 The traditional date at which the Emperor Jimmu comes to throne. (Some scholars move this to 120 B.C.).	Jōmon cultures, probably nomadic; hunting. Shells collected. Pit dwellings. Pottery hibachi with charcoal.
B.C. 300 to A.D. 300	**BRONZE and IRON AGES** A.D. 6 Ponds and canals dug. 135 Reallocations of districts for tax purposes. 270 Emperor Ojin.	Yayoi culture. Agriculture. Metal spears and swords. Wooden implements, including spades. Gold rings. Mirrors, coins, etc. in burials. Some urn burial.
A.D. 300 to 645	**PROTOHISTORIC PERIOD** Referred to as Kōfun or Tumulus Period. 313 Emperor Nintoku. 316 Emperor remits taxes for six years. 478 Shrine of Cereal Goddess moved to Ise. 552 King of Kudara (Korea) sends Buddhist images to Japan. 593 Empress Suiko. **SUIKO PERIOD** 603 Twelve ranks of court nobles established. Shintō shrines probably in operation throughout this period.	A few slaves kept; probably prisoners of war. The serfs were organized into guilds (be) and later into corporations (tomo); most clans owned such guilds. Pit storage buildings. Town dwellings of board and laths. Complicated roofs, but all structures temporary. Iron, bronze, and wooden utensils: rakes, scissors, sickles, harpoons, etc. Enormous tombs and tumuli, an idea perhaps coming from Korea. Ships of fairly advanced construction, with oars and sails.
645 to 668	Emperor Tenchi removes capital to Ōmi. **ŌMI PERIOD** Era of great reforms (Daika).	Tombs much smaller; partly effect of reforms, partly of Buddhist custom of cremation.

Historical Periods and Styles

Art Styles, Art Events and the chief Artists and Works

Vast quantities of the Jōmon pottery of many shapes and with much decoration. Designs made by cord impression, either simple or twisted; rouletting; shell impression; erased cord impression (*surikeshijōmon*); molded handles, etc. Stone and clay earrings, beads and amulets. Clay figurine statuettes. Decorated antlers.

Decorated wooden objects. Bronze bells with designs such as fish, birds and deer. Swords especially, but also spears and halberds, show Chinese and Korean influence. Mirrors mostly of Chinese type but not entirely. Yayoi pottery type, mostly wheel-made but of fewer types than the Jōmon. Designs painted in red appear and especially the "running water" motif.

A few human-headed jars of uncertain significance.

Haniwa pottery, modelled and hollow, either of human beings, animals, or of very complicated model houses. Architecture much more advanced. Tombs contain mirrors, bracelets, swords and their armature. Rather primitive paintings on the walls and screens of tombs—Painted fans used—Armor very fine and of several types, especially of plates of iron held by leather thongs. Leather and metal headpieces. Fine swords on the Chinese pattern; sometimes gilt. Korean trefoil motif is considerably used. Dragonheaded motifs occur on sword pommels and are probably from T'ang style China. Horse trappings become important. Gold and silver inlay quite widely used on metals and gilt-bronze. Little bronze or gold bells for horses are known.

In 607 Hōryuji temple built and many art works put in it which show Gandharan, Indian, Iranian and East Roman influence. Fine Buddhist sculpture in wood, e.g. Yumedono Kwannon at Hōryuji and Guardian Kings or Shitennō (Lokapala). Bronze sculpture of Shaka Trinity by Tori, and Yakushi Trinity; several small Buddhist bronzes—painting was practiced and that of the Tamamushi (inlaid beetle wing) shrine may date here.

The stone carving of the Suiko gives way in this period to the great age of bronze casting. Style of the Sui dynasty of China still present as well as traces of Suiko style.

Dates in Christian Era	Political, Religious, and Literary Events	Social and Technical Events
673 to 710	Emperor Temmu removes capital to Asuka. ASUKA PERIOD The great poet Hitomaro active.	Servitude for debt abolished. Offenses classified. Eleven State Departments for administration set up. Army divided into various corps.
	701 The *Taihō Ritu-ryō* code of laws and regulations completed. 708 Empress Gemmyō ascends the throne.	Minutely detailed census kept. Three kinds of impost: tax (*so*), forced service (*yō*) and tribute (*chō*). *Daigaku* (University) founded for the training of civil servants.
710 to 794	Court removes to Nara: NARA PERIOD Also known as Tempyō Period 712 *Kojiki* compiled. 718 *Nihon-shoki* compiled. 729–760 Ōtomo-no-Yaka-mochi (poet) writing. Growing power of the Fujiwara clan results in plots. 754 The priest Ganjin comes from the T'ang court of China. Many abuses of government in this period as result of plots and some civil war. Outlaws increase. Half Government income goes in works of piety.	Large estates began to fall into private possession and out of the hands of the crown. Because of vast sums spent on religion the treasuries are all impoverished. Officials have to have loans and 1,000 *mon* loan carries interest of 130 *mon* monthly. Thus the cost of living steadily rises. Farmers urged to grow barley and millet on uplands as well as rice in lowlands. Leases of land on "three generations or one life" lead to neglect of agriculture and private ownership of reclaimed land is allowed.
794 to 1184	Capital moved to Heian, pre-sent-day Kyōto. HEIAN PERIOD 805 Saityō returns from China and establishes *Tendai* Buddhism. 806 Kukai returns from China and introduces *Shingon* Buddhism. 847 Priest Ennin returns from China.	799. Cotton seed planted in Nankaidō. 834–850. Buckwheat sown in Kinai. Sorghum, panic grass, barley, wheat, white beans and red beans grown. The *ina-hata* (pad-dy-loom) for drying rice before winnowing comes into use. 5 bushels of rice = 1,000 *cash*; 25 yds. silk = 2,000 *cash*. Capital moved to Kyōto, per-

The T'ang style of China becomes more important as the Korean influence gradually decreases. Sculpture produces more ethereal, slimmer forms with much simplified draperies. The mysticism of former periods dwindles. Notable are the Shaka and Tahō Buddhas in Hasadera temple; these represent the typical plaque form of the period. The beautiful shrine of the Lady Tachibana at Hōryuji shows Indian influence in painting and Chinese in the bronze Amida Triad. Utmost grace of line marks almost all the bronze. Frescoes on the walls of the Kondō of Hōryuji.

Art influences from all over the Asiatic continent at their peak. The bronze Daibutsu of Tōdaiji at Nara, 53 feet high erected and gilded A.D. 749; "eye opening" ceremony not until 752.

Beginning of dried lacquer technique (*Kuanshitsu*), e.g. figure of Bonten (Brahma) $7\frac{1}{2}$ feet high ascribed to Ryōben (689–773). Modelling in clay, e.g. 12 Guardian Kings of Yakushiji, Nara. Wood carvings of Kwannon and also of Gigaku masks; latter preserved in Shōsōin, Nara. Portrait sculpture of the priest Ganjin in the Tōshōdaiji at Nara, in papier mâché.

All these show that the universal "types" of Buddhism elsewhere were, in the hands of the Japanese artist, becoming strongly individualistic. Most of the art tends to be on a large scale; e.g. the *kuanshitsu* 1,000-armed Kwannon in the Tōshōdaiji is 18 feet high.

Scroll, silk, screen and lacquer paintings known.

Earliest wood-block printing.

For the purposes of art history the earlier part of this period is often known as the Jōgan (794–889).

The Tendai and Shingon schools create a mystical monism and in this may be seen a decided shift to Taoist and Vedanta ideas leading, in the ninth and tenth centuries, to a re-discovery of early medieval Hindu art; the influence of this may be seen, for instance, in the six-armed Kwannon at Kanshiji. To meet these mystical and didactic needs there is a marked diminishing of the sense of individuality formerly characteristic of the Japanese artist. Paintings are often mystical and philosophical, such as the Fudō (Guardian King) painted on silk in the Manjuin, or the Red Fudō of Kōyosan monastery. These ideas may be borrowed from Nepalese or early Tibetan art. Colors are chosen for religious

Dates in
Christian
Era

Political, Religious, and
Literary Events

Social and Technical Events

858 Priest Enchin returns from China.

894 Sending of embassies to China, including students, stopped.

905 *Kokin-wakashu*, an anthology of poetry, compiled.

927 The *Engishiki*, a collection of Government regulations and surveys in 50 volumes compiled.

995 Fujiwara Michinaga takes over the Govt.

1004–11 The Lady Murasaki writes the *Tale of Genji*.

1086 *In-sei* (rule by emperors in seclusion inaugurated).

1167 Taira - no - Kiyomori made the Prime Minister.

1175 Hōnen founds the Jōdo sect.

Piracy increases around the coasts. The Fujiwara clan—virtual rulers—enlist help of military nobles, especially Minamoto (Gen.) and start long struggle between these and Taira. (Hei.)

haps to avoid priestly influences. New palace covered 152 acres and took 314,000 workmen/days to finish. New capital laid out like the city of Chang-an, metropolis of T'ang China.

Religion promoted as a means of evading taxes and many unsuitable persons enter the priesthood which slowly grows to military power.

914. Miyoshi Kiyotsura compiles a memorial to the throne and complains of luxury of the times; of the venality of Buddhist and Shintō priests; of poverty and reduced population of rural areas.

Small noble class is pleasure-loving and somewhat effeminate.

The new phonetic scripts of *Katakana* and *Hirigana* introduced but not understood in the rural districts which are still more isolated.

Various attempts made to cope with the complicated forms of *Shōen* (land tenure).

KAMAKURA PERIOD

1185
to
1333

1185 Taira finally overthrown after the long Gem-pei wars and Minamoto no-Yoritomo establishes the government of the Shōgunate.

1202 The priest Eisai spreads the Zen doctrines of Buddhism.

The vassal class increases all through this period.

Society divided into nobles (court and provincial), agriculturalists, industrial workers and traders. Outside of these are the *eta* (those with impurities because of their callings) and *hinin* (the beggars). Near the outcasts are dog-trainers, snake-charmers, symbolism rather than for aesthetic purposes. Names of several great painters come down, such as Kudara Kawanari and Kose no Kanaoka.

Many minor arts flourish. The Lady Sei Shōnagon mentions beautifully scented embroidered dresses and delicately dyed tunics for men, cherry color being prominent. Celadon flowerpots in the palace are also mentioned (Chinese?). The block printing known as *Kyōketi*, begun in the Nara period, is improved and flourishes. The same technique is used to print outlines of pictures on paper which are then delicately colored by hand, such as fan-shaped sutra albums, mostly with genre scenes, but also a few bird and flower subjects. Leatherwork reaches high excellence both in pierced designs and as ground for jewelled inlay.

Resist dyeing of fabrics (batik technique) also taken over from Nara period and designs now more detailed.

Pottery forms softer and more refined than those of Nara period; common glaze is the *haigusuri* (ash glaze); the body of the ware is hard, often grey in color and with small grains of black sand. Fine pottery roof tiles, begun in Nara period, continue to be made and the designs are often simpler and more geometrical. A truly Japanese style of architecture for palaces and nobles' houses now appears, which makes use of formally designed gardens with ponds and islands (*shinden zukuri* style).

Leather and metal designs often copy each other in style, at least in minor ecclesiastical furnishings, both most commonly in openwork; the leather is also colored.

Toward the end of this period the softly glowing colors, softer rounded forms of many objects and the slightly stiffer poses and traceries give way to brighter, gayer color, more refined elongate-sinuous forms and more luxuriant scroll work.

In the latter part of the last age had commenced the movement to build great fortresses (*shiro*) of massive stone blocks fitted together without mortar: this is continued on increasing scale in this period. In keeping with military needs the use of crests (*mon*) becomes more common and heraldic devices turn away from animal forms (formerly totems) to floral and geometrical patterns.

The sweetness and tranquillity associated with the "Pure Land" sects and the works of art they inspired is continued in this period in the Shinran sect but often these characteristics become merely facile and pretty. However, this is counteracted and overborne by the marked rise in popularity of Zen doctrine, which inspires sparse, sober, squarish temples like the Engakuji in Kamakura and, in addition, a portrait sculpture of great starkness and almost overpowering realism. This last probably inaugurated by the father and son Kōkei and Unkei.

	1205 Hōjō Yoshitoki appointed the *Shikken* or regent of the Shōgun. 1219 Minamoto family ruined and political power passes to the Hōjō. 1274 First Mongol invasion suffers disaster. 1281 Second Mongol invasion is wiped out. 1282 Engakuji temple built. The Jōei Code enshrines the whole principles of administration and justice. 1253 The *Hokke-shu* form of Buddhism propagated by the priest Nichiren. A general decentralization of power throughout this period. 1219–22 the Shōkyu struggle wipes out the system of *In-sei*.	acrobats, brothelkeepers and executioners, etc. Sulphur matches come into use and also braziers for heating. 1191. First tea plants introduced. Techniques of steel forging are much improved. Serious attempts made to stop indulgence in luxuries by the military class. *Sake* brewing and the serving of cakes at meals vetoed. *Samurai* have only two meals a day.
1333 to 1397	*Kenmu Restoration.* The Emperor Go Daigo restored by Masashige and Yoshisada and an attempt made to give Imperial House executive power. 1338 Yoshisada dies and Emperor retreats to Yoshino while Takauji, a rival noble, sets up a rival line of Southern Emperors and is made Shōgun.	1341. Takauji sends a trading vessel to the Yuan court of China to import coins. The raising of two crops a year: use of water wheels for irrigation; use of oxen and horses for ploughing now widely established practice.
1398 to 1573	MUROMACHI PERIOD Takauji founds the line of the Ashikaga Shōguns. Period begins as one of luxury of the court of the Shōgun but the country becomes impoverished and nobles leave the capital. Discontent boils	The economic position of the nobles, warriors and priests, hitherto dependent on ownership of land, now on a broader basis. Culture spreads away from the capital to the provinces. In fifteenth century a Dept. of Marine (*amabe*) established to

Here is a return to the purely Japanese individualization of form and an overall emphasis on strongly characterized personality. Portraits are intended to show pre-eminently the intellectual and moral qualities of the sitter. The age has also its own school of painting which turns to new subjects; the old *Yamato-e* style continues but gradually gives place to the Tosa school, which is to continue down to the middle of the nineteenth century. The long horizontal scroll form of composition finds one of the great masters in Sumiyoshi Keion (1166-1237) known from his one scroll which illustrates the *Heiji Monogatari*. Here are great crowds, each figure being well characterized and with some splendid animal painting; everything in the composition of this dramatic work reminds one of the noble grandeur of a great epic poem.

Development in this period of a secular portraiture of immense power, associated with the founder of the Tosa school, Tosa Tsunetaka.

Of minor arts, that of armor and the sword is pre-eminent. Very decorative specimens are made to present to one or other of the many shrines, e.g. Kasuga. Incised and pierced metal work on scabbards.

Butsunichian Kōmotsu Mokuroku (1363), a catalogue of the collection of art objects in the Engaku-ji temple at Kamakura, gives a long list of Chinese paintings and Sung and Yuan Dynasties ceramics and marks the high point of this period of continental influence in art. The quality of mirrors begins to fall off although many show an outer ring of more archaic Chinese design and a central field of pure Japanese pattern.

Nō becomes more popular after the Shōgun Yoshimitsu attends a performance; Nō masks increase in artistry.

Yoshimitsu builds the *Kinkakuji* ("Golden Pavilion") in 1397. It is part Chinese (Sung) and part older Japanese. *Ginkaku-ji* ("Silver Pavilion") erected 1483.

The rise of the tea ceremony and the consequent development of the *Chashitsu* (tea house) occur now.

Art becomes more secular and the Tosa school of painting rises to power with Tosa Mitsunobu (1434-1525?). Three great painters, Jasoku, Sesshu and Sōami live in this period; the work of the first two shows the Chinese landscape

Dates in
Christian   *Political, Religious, and*   *Social and Technical Events*
Era   *Literary Events*

to open warfare in the Wars of Ōnin (1467-9) and in the peasant revolt of Ikpo-Ikki (1488) in Kaga. In 1543 Portuguese come to Tanegashima Island and in 1549 Francis Xavier introduces Christianity.

The latter part of the period is dominated by the rise of several rival war-lords.

Throughout the period the Zen Buddhist culture dominates the society of the nobles and causes the arts to flourish.

Literary works of this period are: *Tsurezure-Gusa* (The Grass of Idleness) by Yoshida Kenkō; many famous Nō plays by Seami and others; also Kyōgen comedies. The art of linked verse (*renga*), e.g. *Minase Sangin* becomes fashionable. *Otogi sōshi* (nursery tales) come into vogue towards end of this period.

develop continental trade. Chinese coins circulate widely and a money economy comes into being. Traders develop *sake* breweries and also loan money on pawned articles. This leads to extensive building of warehouses.

Peasants suffer from excessive taxation; *samurai* are often reduced to poverty and so pawn their belongings but traders flourish and some huge fortunes are amassed. Craftsmen and others form strongly protected guilds (*za*) which are better organized than previously.

There is now the rise of a *chōnin* (merchant) class. The continual use of the *tokusei* (i.e. edict for remission of debts) makes Shōgunate unpopular. Schools and libraries increase in numbers.

1576 to 1600	**MOMOYAMA PERIOD** Oda Nobunaga comes to power and embraces the Catholic faith in order to restrain Buddhist power. Christian missionary efforts increase and the Japanese mission sent to Rome in 1574, whence they had toured Europe, comes home to report. Other *daimyō* send missions to Europe.

1582, Nobunaga assassinated. 1583, Ōsaka castle built by Hideyoshi. He is appointed *kampaku* in 1587 and bans Christianity. 1600, the battle of Sekigahara. The British sailor Wiil Adams comes to | The trends of the last period continue in this. Trade barriers are reduced and the Buddhist Church kept in greater subjection.

The social arts of dancing, singing and instrumental music have a great vogue.

Still further advances in industrial and agricultural techniques. |

in quite distinct Japanese form. Sōami "is a Sesshu bathed in mist and steeped in tenderness."

In ceramics the Seto kilns become pre-eminent and produce *temmoku*-type glazes on jars, dishes, vases, etc. Many show resemblance to Sung Dynasty shapes. Founding of the *Wabi* school of the tea ceremony puts the emphasis on simplicity and there begins a large output of tea bowls founded on the simple, rustic Korean bowls which had been imported. Nearly all the everyday wares are imperfect in some way and all purposely lack "finish". Many other kilns rise to importance, e.g. Bizen.

In metalwork the Buddhist pieces fall off in quality. There is marked evolution in the art of the sword and its fittings. Among the celebrated makers of sword ornaments is Gotō Yujō, founder of the famous Gotō school. Sword guards reach a peak of perfection in the work of Aoki Kaneiye, Myōchin Nobuiye and Umetada Akihisa. The second of these is famous for his armor. Some metalworkers produce various implements for the tea cult, especially tea kettles of great beauty. Many new types of lacquer begin to be made: *Nashiji, togidashi, tsuikoku* and *tsuishu* all become established in this period. Fine pieces are often called *Higashiyama-mono* with reference to the *Higashiyama* palace of Yoshima, who was their patron.

For a time Fushimi becomes the art capital of the empire, as Hideyoshi builds here the great mansions of Juraku and Momoyama, whose lavish decoration requires the services of scores of famous woodcarvers, painters, lacquerers, and metalworkers. The Tosa school develops a type of minutely detailed painting enriched with gold and magnificent colors. The Kanō school of painting also veers to the purely decorative, dusting pure color over a glue base. Kanō painters cultivate as subjects landscapes and birds and also richly and colorfully dressed figures, and rival the Tosa school in their screen paintings. Gold backgrounds are much used. The *sumiye* sketch of former times is neglected. Most of the notable painters of the time are also great lacquerers, such as Kōetsu.

After the death of Hideyoshi his artists and craftsmen move to the courts of the provincial nobles who vie with one another in acquiring art objects. Metalworkers produce lavish fittings of great beauty for the buildings of the times. Sword furniture becomes much richer in decoration, with several new techniques and kinds of inlay evolved. Pottery remains for the most part much more chaste since it is still under the influence of the tea cult which demands simple and subtle form and new gradations of glaze effects. Roof tiles of great elegance are produced. Some potteries, like that of Shino ware, continue to produce designs in the craft tradition.

Japan and introduces several Western techniques. Jan Joosten brings Dutch influence.
War with Korea.
Joruri (ballad drama) and *ayaturi* (puppet drama) are immensely popular throughout the period.

1600 to 1868	**EDO PERIOD**	

EDO PERIOD

1603 The Tokugawa Shōguns become the ruling power.

In this year Okuni, collecting funds for a temple, gives a performance which, according to tradition, developed into the *Kabuki* drama which was to become the dominant amusement of the townspeople of all classes and provide endless themes for the color prints.

1609 Dutch permitted to trade from Nagasaki.

1611 China permitted to trade.

1613 English permitted to trade. Date Masamune sends envoy to Rome.

1615 Fall of the great Toyotomi family.

1623 The English trading station at Hirado closes down.

1635 The system of *Sankinkōtai* established by which the nobles had to spend every other year in Edo and to leave behind their wife and children when they returned to their domains.

The key to the social history of these two centuries of peace is to be found in the rise of the Chōnin class and of a new plebeian culture which had its effects on all cultural activities.

City life develops in many centers during the Genroku era. The five great highways out of Edo (Tōkaidō, Nakasendō, Kōshukaidō, Nikkōkaidō and Ōshukaidō) open up the way for a great interchange of trade which speeds the industrial and commercial development of the country and more and more tends to place the *samurai* and sometimes the *daimyō* in the hands of the *chōnin*.

In the Genroku era several great *gofukuten* (dried goods stores) flourish in the towns and lay the basis of immense fortunes for such families as the Mitsui. An advanced banking system is started and money exchange shops cash Bankers' Orders.

In 1691 the Tokugawa provide forms of relief for their own vassals because of the prevalent distress.

In 1703 the Shōgunal government has to give help to the many destitute in the country.

In textiles, several robes for the Nō drama survive: they often have silk embroidery alternating with bands of imprinted gold. Designs are bold and rich yet chaste and are worked on printed silks, often of understated, glowing colors.

Much of the art of the period foreshadows the taste of the Edo period and is an illustration of the principle that in Japanese art of the later periods the taste of the aristocracy and the styles it engendered quickly worked down the social strata.

The art of this period shows clearly that the Momoyama turned taste away from the *samurai* arts of the Kamakura and Muromachi periods to the plebeian culture of the Edo. There are many minor trends in art that should be investigated. Only a few can be named here.

In architecture the ornate and resplendent style of the Momoyama period is developed into the still more ornate forms of the Tokugawa tombs at Nikko and the palace of Nijō, residence of the Shōguns in Kyōto. The use of *tatami* (mats for kneeling) in the fifteenth century had produced the *shoin-zukuri* style in the Muromachi era, from which developed, during the Edo, the modern Japanese house. The Chinese influence in architecture, as in most other arts, almost disappears, but there are exceptions.

The new movements in Chinese painting in the Ming and Ch'ing Dynasties continue to enter Japan through the Chinese trading post at Nagasaki and a purely Chinese school develops as well as the *bunjingwa* or literary man's school. Confucian studies remain the official entry to learning until well into the eighteenth century and there are periods when Chinese motifs are in vogue as subjects for color prints and *netsuke*, but the influence is a dwindling one and, with the rise of the new class of *chōnin* scholar, the *kokugakusha* or school of classical Japanese learning, as well as renewed interest in Shintō, insures the cultivation of a truly Japanese viewpoint in the arts and learning.

In painting, the Shōgun's court begins by patronizing the Kanō school and the court of the emperor the Tosa school, until the Shōgun Tsunayoshi summons the leading Tosa artist, Sumiyoshi Gukei, to Edo and places him equal in rank to the leader of the Kanō school. The glories of both, however, fast diminish and religious painting, too, for the most part, becomes the work of little more than journeymen-copyists.

In the early seventeenth century the painter Sōtatsu creates a new kind of decorative and highly colored *Yamato-e* painting and this is carried on in the Genroku era, with the same extremely bold designs, by Kōrin (1661-1716). This influence extends into other arts besides painting since Kōrin, like his brother, Kenzan (1663-1743) influences ceramics and lacquer design. A new school of extreme naturalism also appears in the Edo period—the Shijō school—of whom Maruyama Ōkyō (1733–1795) and Mori Sosen (1747–1821) are best known in the West.

1639 Portuguese finally forbidden Japan.	In an attempt to stop the corruption of the *samurai* by the new *chōnin* morality and ways of life the Tokugawa in 1693 issue an edict forbidding all *daimyō* and their own retainers of all ranks from frequenting the Yoshiwara, a problem that is to recur with ever greater urgency during this period.
1653–1724 Chikamatsu Monzaemon, the greatest native dramatist.	
1657 The compilation of the great History of Japan (*Dai Nihonshi*) ordered.	
1637 Shimabara and Amakusa agrarian riots give government an excuse for final suppression of Christianity.	
1688–1704 *Genroku* era, the golden age of Edo culture.	Great rice exchanges are inaugurated at different centers and many of the great traders indulge in wild financial speculation.
1702 The revenge of the 47 Rōnin accomplished and gives rise to endless versions of the *Chusingura* in plays and the arts of Japan.	In the latter part of the eighteenth century and early in the nineteenth century several famines and other great disasters sweep the country.
1720 Embargo on non-religious foreign books lifted.	
1823 Dr. P. F. von Siebold in Japan.	
1853 Commodore Perry comes to Japan and trade treaty follows in 1858.	
1866 The Shōgunate dissolved.	
1802 The *Tokaidō Hizakurige* by Jippensha Ikku published.	
1809 Shikitei Samba writes the *Ukioburo*.	
1814 Bakin begins to write the great *Hakkenden*.	
1829 Ryutei Tanehiko starts the *Inaka-Genji*.	
1827 Death of Issa, the great poet of a new style *Haiku* poetry.	

48

In ceramics a final break with the Sino-Korean influences of nearly a thousand years is brought about by Ninsei and Kakiemon in the seventeenth century. Even so, Chinese traditions are also developed. There is a shift of interest from pottery to porcelain and the results make the Edo period one of the most brilliant in the history of Japanese ceramics.

From the influence of an obscure artist grew the fashionable painting of *Ukiyo-e* and in this style were produced most of the color prints which provide us with a unique documentation of almost all the social life of this era, a documentation which for completeness is probably unmatched in any art in the world.

The textile arts under the extended patronage of the wealthy townsfolk undergoes a most rapid evolution in the mid-part of this period. The *yuzen* method of dyeing, making polychrome patterns possible, now appears, and the intricate *chaya-zome* method of hemp cloth provides most expensive *kimono* for summer wear by the rich. Weaving also progresses, notably in the *karaori* technique which uses gold and silver threads as well as leaves. Embroidery too tends to become more and more elaborate and to attempt a continually greater splendor until, like most of the applied arts at the end of the period, it declines in a welter of over-complication and misapplied ingenuity.

In lacquerware the nouveaux riches show a marked taste for the *maki-e* forms which use gold lavishly.

Netsuke, being used by both *samurai* and *chōnin*, show a wide range of motifs and forms.

49

PART TWO

The arts

HOUSES AND GARDENS

IN Japan, almost all the arts are related ultimately either to dress or to architecture and it is therefore important to know something of the houses as the setting of many of the minor arts and crafts. The climate of Japan has, through the ages, dictated the form of the architecture: the summers are wet and hot and the winters dry and cold, the average rainfall for September in Tōkyō being close to thirty-six inches. This hot, humid climate has necessitated a form of building that will allow the air in summer to pass freely through the rooms and causes most of the buildings, which are of wood, to be raised a considerable distance from the ground on piles. Apart from the special fireproof houses (*kura*), almost all Japanese houses are made of wood, although in a few localities in the provinces, such as Shimotsuke, farmhouses and similar buildings may be of stone.

The house is always intimately related to the garden and has many doors and windows. The ground-plan is capable of much modification since the internal divisions are easily changed. The size of rooms, and indeed of every architectural unit, is standardized and dependent on the number of mats (*tatami*) that it will take to cover the floor. A mat is about six feet by three feet by two inches thick and is made of rice straw bound together and covered with pale green rush. This modular type of building design obviously makes for extreme flexibility. The furniture of the rooms is, for the most part, built-in, creating large uncluttered spaces and a cleanness of line. The main room has a special alcove (*tokonoma*), the floor of which is usually raised a little above that of the room. This alcove probably originated from a small shrine-like niche in which stood a low table in the houses of Zen Buddhists in the Middle Ages. Today the *tokonoma* has on the wall facing the room a hanging scroll (*kakemono*)—either a painting or a piece of fine calligraphy— and perhaps a flower arrangement or an old bronze on its floor.

Japanese room with *tana* or *tokowaki* (shelf-fitted recess) and *shoin* or reading bay.

There are today at least eight types of *tokonoma* and often on one side of this structure will be built another kind of recess fitted with wall-shelves: the *tana* or *tokowaki*. On the other side of the *tokonoma*, and usually at right-angles to it, may be the *shoin* or "reading bay," which is a window—formerly, and still in some instances, a bay window—covered with translucent paper and with a window seat which serves the function of a reading desk, the space underneath being made into a wall cupboard. These may all be very important parts of the design. The other indispensable part of the house is the *engawa* or veranda, which is treated architecturally as a room and serves as a transitional stage between the house and the garden, linking both into one unit.

In building, the Japanese taste is entirely for unvarnished and unpainted wood which is used in the unseasoned state and worked to make the most of the color, polish, grain, and "flash," and put together almost entirely without nails, the main and subordinate parts being held in place solely by the "cut-joint" method, the whole being a masterpiece of carpentry only rivalled by some of the finest cabinet-making of the West. The chief woods used are *Hinoki*

Early form of the *shoin* or
reading bay.

cypress (turning ash-grey with age and usually only used to any
great extent in the houses of the wealthy); *Hiba* wood, which resembles the cypress; *Tsuga* wood, yellowish brown and used in
ordinary building construction; *Sugi* wood, a kind of soft cedar
with a straight grain often used for uprights with merely the peeling
off of the bark by way of preparation; and lastly, the pines, *Aka-
matsu* red pine, and *Kuro-matsu* black pine. In addition to these
timbers there are also used for decorative effect: *Kiri* a very expensive
wood, with a remarkable silver-violet color; *Keyaki* wood; *Momiji*
or *Kaede* wood (two kinds of maple), bright yellow; *Kuwa* wood, a
mulberry with a very fine grain and a light yellow color. Much more
rarely some of the woods earlier imported from India and China are
used for special work. Many kinds of bamboo too are used for
fencing and boarding and many other purposes in both the house
and the garden.

The roofs are a specially charming feature of the Japanese house
and to protect the less durable material of the walls often project
a considerable way beyond the latter. The roof itself is of thatch
or thatch and tiles for farmhouses, shingles for the roof of the
Chaseki (tea-house used for the *Cha-no-yu*), sheet bronze or *Hinoki*

bark for palaces and shrines, and pottery tiles of several designs for dwelling houses and temples. These last are also often characterized by the massive and often ornate brackets for supporting the eaves.

The *Chaseki* occupies a particularly important place in the architecture of the country. It is a structure of the utmost simplicity and refinement designed to give an atmosphere of quiet and secluded rusticity. The tearoom itself is usually only about nine and a half feet square and has the *tokonoma* and a sunken well for a charcoal fire. The entrance (*nijiriguchi*) is so low that each guest has to stoop and creep in—a sign that all rank is laid aside. The eaves are usually wide and the thick translucent paper windows are small and so allow the infiltration of a quiet, soft, mellow light. Sometimes there is a skylight which allows glimpses of the trees in the garden beyond. The garden is no less important in the tea ceremony than the house itself. The outer part (*soto-roji*) has a waiting place (*machi-ai*), where the guests assemble, which has the privy and a water-basin for washing the hands as well as a stone lantern. A path, stone-paved or with stepping stones, leads to a simple wicket gate through which access is gained to the inner garden (*uchi-roji*). This inner garden contains a resting place (*koshikake*) complete with another privy and water-basin at which each guest will rinse his mouth.

The garden art of Japan certainly dates back to the Suikō period and in the Heian era was much developed in relation to the *Shinden-zukuri* style of architecture. In the Momoyama period garden design favored colorful and broad effects, using large stones and trees with bold, vigorous outlines. However, the studied quietness of the tea-house garden was also cultivated and eventually many of its features found their way into ordinary gardens. Gardens are often classified into *hill* gardens (generally with a pond and stream as well) and *flat* gardens with judiciously placed stones, held to represent islands, and trees, but the flat gardens which surround Buddhist temples, particularly in the Kyōto region, often have their design based on a symbolism of more or less profound philosophical import. The Japanese garden traditionally makes the greatest use of stones of unusual shape, trees and bushes pruned to emphasize horizontal masses and the contrasting and ever-changing colors of foliage and vegetation; the colors of flowers usually play a very minor role.

Further Reading

Harada, J., *The Lesson of Japanese Architecture*, London, 1936.

Yoshida, T., *The Japanese House and Garden*, London, 1955.

Tatsui, M., *Japanese Gardens*, Tōkyō, 1934.

Morse, E. S., *Japanese Homes and Their Surroundings*, London, 1886.

Taylour, B. (Mrs), *Japanese Gardens*, London, 1912.

PAINTING AND SCULPTURE

A number of extremely good works on these subjects are easily available, and in them much more information may be found than a book of this size can provide. However, painting enters so intimately into such a number of other arts in Japan that it is necessary to say something about it. Indeed, it is still possible to obtain quite interesting and beautiful paintings in Europe for very much smaller sums than are paid for good prints and for this we have to thank the collectors of Japanese art in France and Britain in "the golden age" of such activity, roughly 1890-1920. Naturally, few such paintings will date before the seventeenth century but there was a great deal of fine work done by the masters of these later centuries and even some fine late copies of older work.

 Painting has been much influenced by calligraphy as is well known, but although calligraphy has been practiced as a fine art in Japan as in China, it has probably never quite reached the rarefied regions that it did in the latter country. The use of *kana* characters made it very difficult to achieve an aesthetic balance between these and the full Chinese ideograms which were employed as well. This was particularly so in *kaisho* (exact or fully written-out characters) and only a little less so in the *gyōsho* (free style) so that most calligraphers exercised their art mostly in the *sōsho* (cursive style) in which the much abbreviated Chinese characters blended more easily with the *hirigana* phonetic signs. Some painters like Musashi (1585-1645) and Shōjō (1584-1639) cultivated calligraphy as much as painting, and this is often to be found among those painters who

54

were much influenced by the earlier Chinese painting or who followed the so-called "literary man's style" (*bunjingwa*) which carried the calligraphic and abstractionist element to extreme lengths. The influence of calligraphy has caused the excellence of much painting to be judged primarily by the force, strength, speed, and modulation of the line and by the delicate play of ink tone which shows amazing variation from dense dull or shining black through ash and silver grey to a mere misted appearance. The ink (*sumi*) is made from the soot of certain plants, such as pine or rush or *Sesamum*, mixed with glue derived often from deer's antlers and hoofs. The tone depends not only upon the way it is applied on the brush but also on the manner in which it is rubbed on the inkstone.

Japanese painting is of various kinds: the *emakimono*, a painting on a long horizontal scroll—usually of silk, but sometimes of paper—made to be unrolled from right to left and looked at, a section at a time; *kakemono*, a painting on paper or silk made to hang vertically; *fusuma-e*, paintings on sliding wall panels; *byōbu-e*, paintings done on screens of either two sections only or a pair, each of six sections; *ema* "votive pictures" made to be donated to temples, most frequently on wood and always with a horse for subject matter; *mitsuda-e*, a painting in oxide of lead with oil on wood, used probably as early as the tenth century, and originating in Persia; it was little used apart from religious work; *gaku* "framed pictures" which, before the late nineteenth century are rare; it is more usual to find various pieces of Chinese-style calligraphy in frames. There are, however, a few paintings on silk in bamboo frames, done about the 1870s onwards, in a curious mixture of *Ukiyo-e* and Western style but of little intrinsic merit. Lastly, there are paintings done on fans (*ōgi-e*), those by Kōrin, Sōtatsu and Chinnanpin being most famous.

Like the Chinese, from whom they borrowed so heavily, the Japanese early codified almost everything about the art of painting. Although the rules were not always rigidly adhered to, they are nevertheless almost always in evidence and a knowledge of them is of great value in directing attention to the technical parts of paintings that must always be evaluated for purposes of dating, authentication, and the like. As an example, there were considered to be four main methods for painting bamboo (always a most important subject in Far Eastern art) and that, in general, artists of the Shijō school pointed the leaves downwards, whereas the Kano school pointed them upwards; as another example may be cited the eight ways of rendering rock ledges, each with such names as "Alum crystals" or "Withered kindling twigs." As with the laws governing such things as harmony and counterpoint in music which help the musician to composition, so these laws of painting acted as guides to certain effects which could be variously combined to capture mood or the inner life of the subject. Even the subjects of Japanese painting, extensive as their range is, were often considered as to their suitability to the various months of the year or to such things as the conveyance of good wishes on a marriage or on attaining the age of seventy.

There is another type of painting of great interest: the so-called "album painting"—a small painting, often, but not always, in ink only, on paper and small enough to be pasted or bound, with others, into a small book. Occasionally, one may come across bound albums of these paintings in which each of the works is by a different artist; these are paintings done by members of an arts club (*renju*) in the eighteenth and early nineteenth centuries. Members were painters, poets, actors, publishers, amateurs or indeed anyone with an interest in the arts and usually these albums were put together to present to a member whom is was desired to honor. Other albums contain poems by different members illustrated by one or two members of the club—usually professional painters—and these usually commemorate some convivial gathering, a visit to the seaside or some notable beauty spot where the club met. In some instances the productions have been put in more permanent form by being published as prints, usually in *surimono* form. Another and more truly corporate form of painting is that in which two artists combined, usually one undertaking the figures and one the landscape: these dual efforts are rare and mostly confined to the Ukiyo-e school.

The schools of Japanese painting are many and the painters are legion, and it would be quite beyond the limits of this work to pass even the main ones in review, but a word or two may be added on the characteristics of those schools of painting most frequently to be met with either in salesrooms or in reproductions.

Buddhist painting was not really a school in the same sense as the other schools, which adhered to a set of canons and rules of technique. Religious paintings were made using several techniques and the treatment and subject matter were often governed by the teachings of some particular sect. Almost certainly the collector will not come across early Buddhist art, almost all of which is in Japan and is listed as a "National Treasure." The later religious art, such as he may from time to time be able to obtain has only small artistic value (unless it is a good copy of some famous early work) but the student may still find such paintings worth having in so far as they illustrate problems of iconography the solving of which will add much to his knowledge of both the Buddhist religion and religious painting.

The *Yamato-e* school is that which first developed in the Heian era and throughout its history it confined itself to purely Japanese themes for its subject matter. More than most other schools in earlier times it enjoyed aristocratic patronage and many courtiers and great priests painted in this style: whole families of painters, generation after generation, followed its canons, perhaps the two most generally known being the Kose and Takuma. It is in a real sense a school of illustrators, since the themes most often reproduced were taken from the medieval romances and histories. Its techniques included the use of soft, harmonious colors and fine hair-like lines; most characteristic was the use of single fine lines to denote eyes and noses. During the Momoyama period it went into a complete decline but was revived in the late Edo period and any works the collector will meet with will belong either to this last phase or else be copies of earlier masterpieces.

The Tosa school arose in the Muromachi period and, like the *Yamato-e*, painted the traditional subjects to which it added in later times the illustration of some folk-tales, e.g. *Urashima*. Later still, purely decorative subjects, such as birds and flowers, and in the Momoyama era, genre subjects of a kind that brought the school near to the commencement of the *Ukiyo-e*. All paintings of this school are done on a special kind of paper; they are detailed and even minute in treatment, use brighter colors and a stronger and more modulated line than the *Yamato-e*.

The Suiboku school worked almost exclusively in black and white (*sumi-e*) with extremely strong brush-strokes, and drew their subjects for the most part from the range of Chinese paintings although, even in landscape, these tended to break away from the generalized landscape treatment of the Chinese in favor of the reproduction of an actual Japanese scene—some lake or mountain range. Very occasionally light colors are washed in—yet another Japanese characteristic. This was the school so much favored by the *samurai* and the priests, especially those of the Zen sect. It is not uncommon to find on the *kakemonos* of this school inscriptions—frequently poetical—in praise of the work itself and written often by other hands: this was another Chinese characteristic.

In the fifteenth century arose the Kanō school of painters, originally a marriage of the two last schools. The earlier masters confined themselves to black and white, but later introduced color into their work. The influence of the northern Chinese school was strong at first but Sōami (died 1525) followed the softer "misty" style of the Chinese painter Mu-ch'i, and a larger part of the technical equipment of the Kanō school was founded on a study of the paintings of that master. Boldness, the vital force of the brush-stroke, and the immense range of ink tone are the marks of this school, most of whose works were done on silk although some artists worked on paper as well.

The Sōtatsu school (founded by an artist of that name) and its offshoot, the school of Kōrin, is one of the easiest for the beginner to recognize. Here the aim is frankly decorative and the treatment often one of great breadth, boldness and strength with a gorgeousness of color added. Flowers and birds are the most frequent themes, often one kind of subject, such as waves or irises, completely dominating the whole composition. Quite frequently there is a widespread use of gold-leaf in the paintings of this school.

The *Ukiyo-e* school is the one principally concerned with the color prints and with the life and interests of the *chōnin* class. Since the work of this school will be reviewed under the section on color prints it is only necessary to add here that paintings too were done in this style which was essentially a product of the Edo era.

Also of that period was the Maruyama or Shijō school (sometimes treated as two separate schools) which turned its efforts to a new kind of realism based on certain realistic paintings of the Sung and Yuan Dynasties of China. This is the school that most immediately appeals to the Western collector, who spontaneously marvels at the treatment of such things as hair and feathers and whose admiration is won by the often unusual composition, realistic pose and perfect placing. When the niceties of brush-stroke have come to be appreciated from the traditional point of view, however, the early praise for the productions of this school becomes somewhat modified. Most of the masters of this school are happiest with trees and animals (although Ōkyō, the founder, is known to have painted for a time with Western perspective and even undertook a few pornographic nudes) and they use for the most part short massed brush-strokes with little regard for the continuity of line such as the Kanō school mostly maintained. Hair was done in one of two ways; either the ordinary brush (*fude*) was spread wide so that each hair drew a line or the broad brush (*hake*) was made use of to obtain such things as a broad treatment of fur or feathers.

Little needs to be added concerning sculpture since that which the collector will mostly acquire will be in the form of *Okimono* or bronze work or a rare finer piece of wood-carving. Mention has been made of the great sculptural masterpieces of earlier times, all of which are either objects concerned with the decoration of temples or used as part of the Buddhist ritual or else are part of the series of marvelous portrait statues produced under the influence of that religion. After the Kamakura era the art of Buddhist sculpture declined sadly, so much so that when Hideyoshi in the sixteenth century ordered a large statue of Buddha, Sōtei Hōin and Sōin Hōgen, the two leading sculptors of Nara, the ancient center of the art came to Higashiyama, but their work was so poor that it could not be used. There was an increased demand for Buddhist images when, in 1605, Hidetada ordered every household to have one; carvers no doubt flourished and multiplied for a time but the demand was soon satisfied and many of the new carvers turned their attention to the carving of *netsuke*, ornamental fan-lights (*ramma*) and similar objects.

Sometimes Buddhas in the dry lacquer technique of the Kamakura period may be found and occasionally these are of good quality; however the beginner should be warned that many are composition imitations. At times good carved shrines are available at fairly modest prices, but important signed pieces of wood-carving are rare, although from around 1850 to 1880 members of the Takamura school (especially Takamura Hōun, T. Tōun and T. Kōun) reached a certain degree of excellence. By the middle of that period, however, their work was sacrificing such virility as it had to a naturalistic prettiness. Of about the same period is some fairly good bronze sculpture, some of which rises to minor importance. It is sometimes signed with the name of Seikokusai.

Further Reading

Bowie, H. P., *On the Laws of Japanese Paintings*, San Francisco, 1911, and later editions.

Paine, R. T., and Soper, A., *The Art and Architecture of Japan*, London, 1955.

Kenji Toda, *Japanese Scroll Painting*, Chicago, 1935.

Binyon, L., *Painting in the Far East*, London, 1923 and later editions.

Kenji Moriya, *Die Japanische Malerei*, Weisbaden, 1953.

Fenollosa, E., *Epochs of Chinese and Japanese Art*, New York, 1921 and later.

Warner, L., *Japanese Sculpture of the Suiko Period*, New Haven, 1923.

Warner, L., *The Craft of the Japanese Sculpture*, New York, 1936.

Warner, L., *The Enduring Art of Japan*, Harvard, 1952.

Tokuzo Sagara, *Japanese Fine Arts*, Tōkyō, 1949.

Seiichi Taki, *Three Essays on Oriental Painting*, London, 1910.

Omura, *Tōyō Bijutsu Taikwan*, Tōkyō 1908 ff. (Excellent reproductions of all schools and periods of both sculpture and painting.)

Gray, B., *Japanese Screen Painting*, London, n.d. (1956–?).

Morrison, A., *The Painters of Japan*, 2 vols., London, 1911. (Still an important critical work.)

Watson, W., *Sculpture of Japan from 5th to 15th cent.* London, 1959. (Especially good for Nara and Kamakura periods).

Netsuke. A cicada on a leaf under which is a large spider. Late eighteenth- early nineteenth century.

NETSUKE AND OKIMONO

The function of the *netsuke* was to act as a toggle or counterpoise at the opposite end of the cord which held the *inrō* or some other small accessory which itself dangled from the girdle. Originally a small gourd performed this duty as well as acting as an amulet and, later, as a flask for *sake* (*hyōtan*), such flasks having been much prized in Japan. This custom seems to have arisen in the sixteenth century and in the early Edo period this and other small articles were suspended from the girdle by a ring (*obiguruwa*) which was sometimes of ivory. More distantly an origin may be found in the Chinese girdle-toggle which itself was perhaps derived from a part of the early Chinese ceremonial girdle pendants.

At the end of the seventeenth century the custom of hanging *inrō* and money purses (*kinchaku*) on a cord from seals imported from China and pierced with a hole to take the cord, was well established and an increasing number of otherwise unemployed carvers turned their attention to these little objects. For some time *netsuke* do not seem to have been worn by the *samurai* classes but were cultivated by the merchants who came to prize them and the tobacco pouch (*tabako-ire*) much as the *samurai* prized their swords. The famous *Sōken Kishō* by Inaba Michitatsu (1781), although it deals mostly with lacquerers and metalworkers, also lists fifty-seven carvers of *netsuke* and among these a Shintō priest, several Buddhist priests, a Kanō-school painter, carvers of traceried fan-lights (*ramma*) and of trellis-work (*ranmashi*) and from this we may see what kind of men the early carvers were who first turned their attention to *netsuke*.

The many materials of which *netsuke* were made are given in the notes on materials but they may be classified also by the form in which they were made. Most of these forms were present in the early days, but at first most *netsuke* were made of wood although this does not by itself date a piece since wood continued to be used occasionally until the latest period of their manufacture. First, in point of view of the numbers represented in Western collections, are the *katabori netsuke*, carved as figures, more or less in the round; then come the *manju netsuke*, which are round or square bun-shaped ones made either in one piece or in two matching pieces which are pulled together when the cord which runs through them is tightly drawn; these usually have the design in low relief or, more rarely, engraved on them; another variety, the *ryusa netsuke*, shaped like the *manju*, is hollow inside and carved in open tracery work. The *kagamibuta*

Netsuke in *Hinoki* cypress wood. A toad. Signed: Shuzan (i.e. Yasusada Shuzan of Echigo province). Late eighteenth-early nineteenth century.

Netsuke in cherry wood. Figure of a Shōjō sleeping off the effects of *sake*. Signed: Ikko. Late eighteenth century.

form is really a shallow bowl-shaped *netsuke,* in wood or ivory, with a metal lid which may have the design either chased on it or inlaid. The *sashi netsuke* is an elongate one usually in wood, and in earlier times as much as seven inches long, having a hole at one end through which the cord passed, while the opposite end was stuck in the girdle. The *ichiraku netsuke* was woven of rattan or wire and shaped into the form of a gourd or similar object. This kind may have been one of the earliest—at least in some regions of the country— since the author has seen an early example, of peasant production, in the form of a *jakago,* which was a rough cylindrical basket of bamboo, filled with stones and lowered into fast-flowing rivers where, resting against the bank, it prevented soil erosion. Such roughly made or crudely carved peasant *netsuke* are fairly common and often have at worst a naïve charm and, at best, a great power. The collector would do well to look for these, but he must be sure to distinguish them from the coarsely made and horribly stained city productions of later days, intended for the tourist trade. Other and rarer kinds of

63

netsuke exist such as those which served as ash-trays (*suigararake*), an abacus or counting frame (*soroban netsuke*) or as sundials, "penknives," candlesticks, telescopes or magnifying glasses. Here we can only deal with those that were carved in wood, ivory or some other material and not with those made of metal, pottery, porcelain and similar substances which classify as *netsuke* only by their function.

It is important to distinguish the types of carving and of these one can recognize the following: *sukashi-bori*, or carved open-work; *ukibori*, or carving in relief, which was usually reserved for the detail of dresses or the rendering of surface texture of various natural objects; *itto-bori* (lit. "one-cut carving") which gave a series of simple planes, boldly cut as though by great chisel thrusts. This last was a practice much used by the Hida school and sometimes such pieces have on them the words "*iichi shiichi*" or "*ichishi*," which are not signatures but terms for the technique employed. The word *katakiri*, frequently met with, refers to the kind of engraving which uses lines of variable depth and width. *Kebori* is applied to an engraving of hair-like lines of great fineness and equal width and depth, particularly used on the map *netsuke* of Nanka and for the poems often found engraved on the work of the school of Iwami. In addition to these processes, various kinds of inlaying were practiced for different effects and in some later pieces staining was resorted to, the juice of the *kuchi-nashi* berry (*Gardenia florida*) being used for this purpose. Those made in the shape of the so-called *Nara-ningyō* dolls were painted in watercolor and a few kinds may be found painted in lacquer.

Meinertzhagen, the author of the definitive work on the schools of *netsuke* carvers, divides them into the following: the Ōsaka carvers who began production in the eighteenth century and who then carved mostly in wood but, as supplies became more plentiful, turned increasingly to ivory and produced such great carvers as Hidemasa, Hidetada, Masakazu and Masatsugu in the early nineteenth century, at which time another school of *manju* carvers founded by Kōgiokusai Naomitsu started production in the same city. All these carvers worked in ivory. Meinertzhagen especially singles out for praise the work of two late masters of this school,

Ōhara Mitsuhiro, who was noted for his *katakiri* engraving and signed usually with some sort of *kakihan* after his name, and Kwaigioku Masatsugu, who was carving down to 1892, producing many different things besides *netsuke* and who made an immense reputation for his extremely elaborate *sukashi* work. Another school was that at Kyōto; four of the groups active in that city traced back to carvers mentioned in the "Sōken Kishō" and a later one had a tradition of carving going back to the carver Kagetoshi, noted for figure groups and landscapes in *sukashi-bori*. However, Kyōto was not to produce a large number of carvers—perhaps the capital of the Imperial court was not as good a market as Tōkyō (Edo) where the largest number of rich merchants had their business. Meinertzhagen has cleared up many of the problems of the relationships between the numerous carvers who were active during the nineteenth century in Tōkyō, and they include the most interesting group of the Deme school—for centuries noted carvers of masks—some of whose followers turned to mask *netsuke* and continued their activity throughout the Edo period.

In Nagoya, capital of the province of Owari, there flourished a school of noted *netsuke* carvers, almost all of whom worked in wood of which the favorite varieties were boxwood (*tsuge*)—a wood that grew to perfection in the surrounding districts—cherry (*sakura*), traditionally first used by Miwa of Edo in the eighteenth century, persimmon wood (*kaki*), ebony (*kokutan*) and *keyaki* wood (*Zelkova acuminata*). The larger part of the work of this school represents animals, either vertebrate or invertebrate, with a few plant forms and mask *netsuke*. Many provincial masters from Ise and Mino moved to Nagoya, one of whom, Tanaka Minkō, introduced the technique of inlaying parts of the design in ivory and metal and coloring the wood to accentuate certain features. Tōkyō certainly produced the greatest number of *netsuke* carvers and it is almost exclusively from here that there came in late Edo times and in the following modern period the immense numbers of small ivory groups, facile and effete even if technically creditable, which make up the bulk of the *netsuke* found in antique shops and the glass specimen cases of an older and less wise generation of their admirers.

The only remaining *netsuke* carvers of serious artistic standards

65

still active today are Sōsui and Shōkō, both pupils of Sōko Morita (1879-1935) and both working in ivory. There are, however, a few good-quality wood *netsuke* or *netsuke*-form carvings made today for the western market, but these are not primarily in the Japanese taste. Of late date also are some good-quality "coral divers" of ebony, coral and ivory inlay, but there are also a large number of ivory carvings of contemporary or recent date which are really made for the tourist trade and were never intended for use. The favorite subjects for these pieces are children with baskets, hares, Sennin drinking, Hotei drinking, Fukurokuju with a Daruma-toy, and peasants with cockerels. Certain pieces are copied by Chinese carvers in Hong Kong and imported by Western dealers and some of the above subjects are made in plastic in Italy and Hungary and sold, not only throughout Europe, but also in Japan! All these forgeries are not difficult to tell with even a little practice, but there are others that are more difficult and the fact that almost identical examples of a given theme exist does not render one of them a forgery since it was part of the normal procedure of instruction for the pupil to copy the master's designs and for these to be sold on the legitimate market. Apart from artistic merit, style and choice of subject, it is not easy to validate any given piece. With regard to the last of these, the following points can be made: In the eighteenth century the usual subjects were seals, Sennin, mythological animals (most often similar to those that figure in Chinese folklore as well as Japanese), doll and puppet *netsuke* (*Nara-ningyō*), hermits, and masks. The greater part of this work is in wood with only a few pieces in ivory, most of the latter being the work of masters who specialized in this medium. The nineteenth century saw an immense increase in the use of ivory for *netsuke*, especially for those with fine detail and having human figures or gods for their subject, but in the first half of the century there was also a large output of forms such as snakes, insects, shells, frogs, rats and hares, and most frequently these were in wood. Toward the end of the nineteenth century *netsuke* became more elaborate and detailed and to meet the naïve wonderment of Westerners these were finally produced with a number of finely carved projecting parts which, had they ever been worn, would have broken off in a few months. Other points that are produced by age are the wear at the cord holds (*himotōshi*), differential fading, and the patina which wood and ivory take on when in contact with the secretions of the sebaceous glands of the skin. All these, however, can be faked by the determined forger and, as prices rise, incentives become the greater. Also the student may be puzzled by the existence of two classes of *netsuke* that existed at all times; the first, a small, light, neatly made and often "chunky" or cone-shaped one and the second, a larger, heavier, pyramidal, cylindrical or irregularly shaped form. The first seems to have been used with *inrō* (and several *netsuke* carvers are known to have made *inrō* and would no doubt have designed the *netsuke* to match them) and the second for *tonkotsu* (a large tobacco box of wood) or some other heavier article.

From the late figure group *netsuke*, whose increased production was encouraged by Western demand, arose the *okimono* (a carving to stand in an alcove); even when small these lack the cord-holes of the *netsuke*, but they are usually to be recognized by their much larger size and highly detailed workmanship. They were often made to the order of some Western patron of the carver's who might even provide a *netsuke* model with instructions to render it on a much larger scale and, almost always, in ivory. Some undoubtedly were intended as original works of art and this is especially so with the work of Ishikawa Kōmei (mid-nineteenth century) and his pupils, such as Riōmei, all of whom were responsible for very detailed and highly naturalistic work; others again, it seems, were signed with the name of some noted *netsuke* maker such as Gyokusai or Okatomo, often, as in the last instance, eighteenth-century masters; yet others have signatures which are not known to occur on *netsuke* and it seems likely that these specialized in this kind of work. It is probable too that a considerable group of those who were producing work of higher quality were members of the Ōsaka school if one is to judge by their names. Although there was much poor work in *okimono* carving produced in Tōkyō there was a school of good carvers whose names are also found on such things as writing cases and pipe cases as well and who may have originated in the studio of the late eighteenth-century carver Minkoku, who was also noted for his fine *netsuke* in both wood and ivory.

Further Reading

Okada, Y., *Netsuke, a miniature art of Japan*, Tōkyō, 1951. (Very informative and a corrective to some European work.)

Ryerson, E., *The Netsuke of Japan*, London, 1958. (An excellent guide to the subjects of *netsuke* and very well produced.)

Jonas, F. M., *Netsuke*, 1st ed. London and Kobe, 1928; 2nd ed. Tōkyō, 1960. (Deals with other subjects besides *netsuke*.)

The three above works are excellent and each shows considerable erudition in this field. Surprisingly, they do not duplicate their material as much as may be supposed, and a student should at least see all three even if he cannot possess them.

Meinertzhagen, F., *The Art of the Netsuke Carver*, London, 1956. (The most complete work on the history and schools of carvers in English and by the foremost living authority in the Western world on this subject.)

Brockhaus, A. E., *Netsuke*, Leipzig, 1924. (In German, still a standard work but out of print and very expensive.)

Roth, S., *Netsuke*, Goteborg, 1933, in Swedish and English.

Ueda Reikichi, *Netsuke no Kenkyu* (The Study of Netsuke), 2nd ed. Ōsaka, 1943. (An important work in Japanese and the source of most biographical material and with a useful list of signatures and illustrations.) English translation, 1962.

Bunke, H. G., *Netsuke*, Braunschweig, 1959.

Hull-Grundy, A., *Netsuke by the Carvers of the Iwami School*, London, 1961, privately published.

MASKS AND DOLLS

It is probably not too much to claim that in the art of the mask Japan is pre-eminent of all the countries of the world. By no people in the world was such an extraordinary subtlety achieved in these objects as in the Nō masks of that country. Almost all the masks carved in Japan were, in fact, used either in various forms of dancing or in the drama and it is perhaps because little is known of these in the West that interest is not more widespread among the collectors of Europe where mask collecting has had only intermittent popularity.

The earliest form of the native dances, the *Kagura*, produced in front of Shintō shrines, probably had no masked performers, but the masks that persist and, indeed, in a few instances are still in use in *Kagura* dances today, are borrowed and decadent versions of Nō and Kyōgen masks. Special forms of what are sometimes loosely called *Kagura* dances are the *Iwato* or congratulatory New Year dances in which masks are sometimes worn, the commonest being a lion mask. Somewhat allied to these, but most probably with a multiple origin, are the *Matsuri* or processions in honor of some Shintō deity: often these consisted of a float or floats each carrying dancers or musicians, the former being sometimes masked, and halberd-crowned cars (*hoko*) on which scenes were depicted by dolls. There is a manuscript of 1635 which notes that in that year a peddler of salt in the town of Otsu danced at the *Shinomiya matsuri* in a raccoon mask. These raccoon masks are still fairly common but they seem mostly to be the product of peasant art and no doubt some have been handed down for centuries although most are of late eighteenth- or early nineteenth-century workmanship. In early times, too, *Dengaku* was under the patronage of nobles and no doubt had artistic masks in some of its forms as did the comic *Sarugaku* (monkey music) but while some of these dance-dramas were absorbed into the Nō plays others dropped back again into the world of rustic festivities from which they came and it is these that have produced the *Dengaku* and *Sarugaku* masks that have come down to us; crude in character, heavy, and showing only the simplest craftsmanship in carving, they are really only of ethnographical interest and perhaps of historical importance as antecedents of the Nō plays.

Gigaku, a bucolic dance-drama with great similarities to British "hobby horse" village plays, came to Japan in the sixth century and used large, heavy masks in glowing color, with deep carving, designed to cover most of the head. These masks represented set characters, several with long noses, long ears or other accentuation, and also a bird mask (*karura*) and a lion mask (*shishi*). *Gigaku* has long been

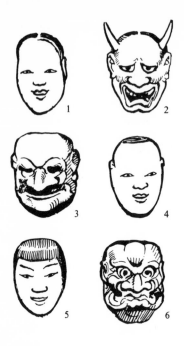

A group of Nō and Kyōgen masks. 1. Koomote, a young girl: the mask for this part is regarded as the greatest test of the art of the mask carver. 2. Hannya, a demon. 3. A Kyōgen comic mask. 4. Buaku mask (kyōgen); a comic version of Ōbeshimi in the Nō. 5. A Kyōgen mask of a young girl. 6. Ōbeshimi mask; an angry flying goblin.

extinct, supplanted by *Bugaku*, a series of artistic dances of serious intention imported from Asia by way of China, some of which made use of masks. The oldest surviving ones are eleventh century, and on the whole they tended to decline steadily in design and workmanship, but even the late ones show an undeniable artistry. *Bugaku* masks are symbolic and in no sense realistic as are the *Gigaku* ones and while the latter have the hair carved or sometimes real hair inset on the mask, the latter for the most part have the hair painted on and the mustache and beard sometimes end in stylized spirals. *Bugaku* masks are light and small in size and have movable parts, especially the eyes and chin, and the overall decorative intent is always obvious in treatment and design. The *Gyōdō*, sometimes known as *Neri-kuyō*, is a ceremony in which some Buddhist figure or icon is taken in procession through the streets and shown to the people or, in a different form may be a dramatic representation of religious scenes. Various Buddhist figures are represented in both of these by actors with masks symbolic of various celestial beings or

Buddhist "saints" and, in the processional form *Tengu* (long-nose beings) and *Shishi* (lions) acted by humans with these masks, lead the ceremony. All *Gyōdō* masks are imitative and have closed mouths and openings for the yes and are usually rather heavy. *Oni* (devil) masks are not uncommon; they show great muscular protuberances indicative of superhuman strength and are usually colored green or red. These were used in the *Tsuina* ceremony in which devils were driven out on the first day of spring by scattering beans. Formerly the one driving them out (*Hososhi*) wore a mask with four eyes and held a halberd, but this practice seems to have died out several centuries ago.

The triumph of the Japanese art of the mask was in the creation of those used in the production of the Nō dramas and Kyōgen comedies: these masks in the fourteenth century became the specialization of schools of carvers who passed down their precepts from generation to generation. The Nō masks are of light carved wood and made to fit the face only, tying behind the head with silk cords. The wood was lacquered various colors—usually white, but also brown, brownish-red (for demons, such as *Hannya* and *Kobeshimi*), red (often for infants and young boys, such as *Chojo*), and very occasionally gold (*Kurokami*) for gods or superior beings. Although they have no movable parts at all they do sometimes have hair added to them and always the expression is profound, subtle or mysterious, the mask seeming to take on a super-personality of its own; with many of them the carving is such that as the actor turns his head to or from the light, lifting it up and down, there seems to appear momentarily an inner radiance or a deep inturned melancholy. It is here above all that we may find in the work of the great carvers the quality of *yugen*. Kyōgen masks, often with the mouth a little open showing the tongue or a row of broken teeth, invite laughter; they are frankly caricatures of recognizable types and, by implication, they hold up to ridicule the follies, stupidities and cupidities of erring humanity. In these comedies even such gods as Ebisu are treated with a certain familiarity—shown too in the masks —and nowhere in the whole range of these plays is there a beautiful woman such as is found in the Nō dramas.

Dolls are made of a variety of materials such as porcelain, bronze, clay and carved wood. Dolls (*ningyō*) were used not only by children, but also for purposes of magic and as amulets in more primitive times. Later they developed into the form of puppets which originally appeared as illustrations to the *jōruri*, a kind of ballad-drama which evolved from public recitals of the two great epics, the *Heike Monogatari* and *Taiheike*. In the sixteenth century appeared the *Ayatsuri* (manipulation), a drama acted by dolls which were at first made of clay; under the influence of Satsuma Jōun, in the first half of the seventeenth century, they were replaced by carved wood puppets. In the course of time these became amazingly complex, requiring two manipulators each and were so beautifully designed and made that their personalities were capable of arousing the emotions of the audience in a manner that equalled that of the live actors of the Kabuki. The performances of these miracles of puppetry were given at special doll theatres, the Ningyō Shibai. Few examples have found their way into Western collections and fine old specimens are the treasured possession of a few native collectors.

Some of the older clay dolls produced in rural districts are well worth the attention of collectors and even those being produced today in some places, such as Fushimi and Hakata, have considerable aesthetic quality. Dolls carved in wood are of several kinds: some represent nude boy babies, generally with unusually large heads in the older examples; these are called *gosho-ningyō*. Then there are the *Nara-ningyō*—another art-form of boldly carved and painted dolls representing Nō actors—of which the foremost sculptor was Morikawa Tōen of Nara in the late Edo period. *Saga-ningyō* were dolls painted in bright colors and the *kimekomi-ningyō* were carved in wood with pieces of cloth glued to them—those of the late Edo and Meiji periods often show great artistry. Several other kinds exist including all the charming ones used for the Dolls' Festival; these come nearer to the Western idea of a doll. Finally, there is a primitive folk-art product, the *kokeshi*, lathe-turned and carved and appealingly painted in bright colors and of almost innumerable patterns and sizes which, although common, is well worth collecting before the traditional designs become sophisticated and mass-produced.

Further Reading
Yamada Tokubei, *Japanese Dolls*, Tōkyō, 1959.
Noma Seiroku, *Masks*, Tōkyō, 1957.
Figdor, 'Japanische Masken', *Theatre Band*, 1, No. 5 (1909).
Perzynski, F., *Japanische Masken: Nō und Kyōgen*, 2 vols., Berlin, 1925.
Inouye, K., 'Dolls as Art', *Japanese Magazine*, Bd. 10, pp. 9–14, 1919–20.
Gehri, H., *Nō-Masken*, 1er Bd. 8, pp. 549–54, Kunst und Kunst, 1910.

LACQUERWORK

Lacquer is derived, as the result of quite complicated techniques, from the sap of the tree *Rhus vernicifera* (Fam. *Anacardiaceae*), the essential constituent of which is urushiol, a fairly complex hydrocarbon. In its pure state it is called *kurume urushi*, when sifted *seshime urushi*, and after mixing with sulphate of iron to give the lustrous black color which much of it has, *kuro urushi*. The techniques for working it were developed in quite early times (tradition says mid-third century and certainly by the sixth century) and the natural product of Japan had the advantage of being of better quality than that of China. The effects of this early perfection of lacquering in Japan had several repercussions in history: the art was held in higher esteem in that country than in China or elsewhere in Asia and its widespread use at an early date may have held back the development of ceramics. The finest art lacquerware of Japan was always a luxury article and extremely expensive—partially because of the long and complicated processes involved in its production and partly because of the hundreds of man-hours of the highest skilled labor which had to go into the making of even the smallest article—and, although there was a demand for it in Europe and other Asian countries at an early date, there was, until the latter part of the nineteenth century, a reluctance to pay the prices demanded. These conditions caused the Japanese to produce, after about 1870, a lacquer industry designed to supply a much cheaper and obviously inferior article suited to the Western demand. The essential difference

73

is clearly to be seen in the following incident: in 1874 the paddle steamer, *Le Nil*, carrying the objects destined for the Japanese Government exhibit in the Vienna Exhibition, sank in Yokohama bay; when finally salvaged after very prolonged immersion in sea water, the older lacquers were found to be completely unharmed, but the more modern products were ruined. Lacquer is perhaps unique among the crafts of a civilized people in being one that rose to the status of a fine art in Japan, yet was consistently applied, throughout its whole history, to objects of everyday use.

Lacquer has been applied to articles made of a large range of substances. Woods, whether of the cypress, *keyaki*, cedar, gingko, chestnut or magnolia tree (*hō*) (the last used especially by the lacquerers of Niigata and Yonezawa) as well as many others were used; plaited bamboo; ceramic wares (first used so in the Momo-

Kōgō (Box for incense), shaped like two clam shells and used for playing the *Kai-Awase* game. One shell decorated with a fan and gourd-vine, symbols of the chapter "Yugao" of the Genji Monogatari; the other with a spray of cherry blossom.

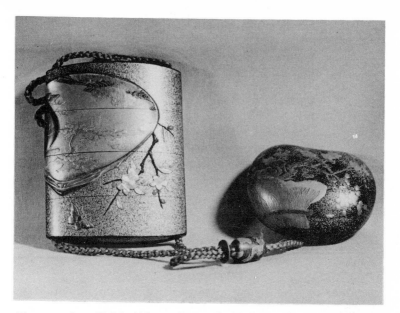

Three-case *Inrō*. *Kinji* (gold lacquer) ground with design of *takamaki-e* of two *kinji* shells with a river flowing under pine and wisteria trees. Length 2⅜ inches. Width 2¼ inches. *Ojime*. Bronze. Vase shaped with an inlaid design of dragon and clouds. *Netsuke*. Reniform *manju*-shaped lacquer, *nashiji* on black ground with a design of a plum tree leaning over a hedge in spring.

yama period); cow, deer or wild boar hide (first used in the Nara period); sheets of a tough paper pasted over a wooden mold to give the shape; similarly treated sheets of hemp cloth (*soku*)—a technique perfected at Nara—and that most typical of all lacquer products in Western collections, the *inrō* (a case for seals or, later, medicines) seems to have been constructed—or at least one very common type does—of layers of a papery fabric made of the paper-mulberry fibres bonded together with dried and powdered river mud, strengthened with very thin strips of coniferous wood and impregnated with raw lacquer. It also seems likely that these composition *inrō* were made on a very slightly tapered wood mold to allow of their easy removal in sections. However, the lacquer coatings of some *inrō*, as of some other lacquered articles, were made directly on to carved wood.

There are a great many kinds of lacquer, but five main families of lacquered surface may be recognized:

1. Black.
2. Gold.
3. Red.
4. Other colors.
5. Incrusted or inlaid lacquer.

Of these red lacquer (*tsō urushi*), prized by many connoisseurs for its marvellously vibrant color, is always carved and, unlike the practice in China, the Japanese seem only to have made very small pieces of this kind. It is also peculiar in that there is now accumulated evidence that many red *inrō* and other articles were made in China and imported into Japan, the styles of these being distinctly Chinese, while the designs of the Japanese artists who worked in this technique—artists such as the *netsuke* and *inrō* maker Hokei and the famous lacquer artist Zonsei—remained Japanese although the subjects of most of this carved red lacquer are Chinese. Perhaps the commonest types of lacquer are those in which the design is in gold on a black ground, the design being either engraved and chased (*chinkin-bori*), flat or in very low relief (*hira maki-e*), or raised above the black ground (*takamaki-e*). *Raden*, the carrying out of parts of the design in a kind of *collage* of shell or metal (usually pewter or silver of which the school of Kōrin were very fond) is also quite common. Another method of carrying out a design is known as *togidashi*, in which the subject is drawn by sprinkling gold or silver powders on a slightly wet top coat of lacquer; when dry, it is covered with another coat of lacquer and, finally the whole is rubbed down with charcoal until the design appears; this gives an appearance of great richness to the finished product. Colored lacquers other than red or black or gold are not so common and are most frequently used in conjunction with the *togidashi* technique especially to represent feathers and similar objects on a black ground. A peculiar brown lacquer is sometimes used to imitate that of old Seto ware pottery and there is a very rare dove-grey of most beautiful appearance whose use may date from the eighteenth century. Two uses of colored lacquer must have especial mention; that called *mokume* makes use of two (often red and black) or more colors applied in a wavy fashion which, when finally ground down, gives the impression

Four-case *Inrō*. *Fundame nashiji-nuri* ground; decoration in *takamaki-e* and mother-of-pearl of butterflies and lantern bugs. Signed: Koma Yasutada. Nineteenth century.

of a highly colored wood of very marked grain; the second and more important emphasizes carving; in this the design is slightly raised by carving and covered with red and green lacquer in the very early pieces, or with red and black in those dating from Tokugawa times. The whole is covered with black lacquer and then ground down with fine powders to show the underlying designs; this is known as *Kamakura-bori* and is said to have been invented by Kōben in the Kamakura period. *Guri* lacquer is another highly favored form that uses colored lacquers (usually red and black and sometimes with yellow or green); these are applied in alternating coats and when dry a simple scroll form design is carved through them with deep cutting showing the different colored layers. A form of this was used in Kamakura times and in this red and green were used in layers in such a way that a design could be cut showing red flowers with green foliage. A somewhat similar effect, but carried out with a rather

77

different technique, is found in Sung Dynasty Chinese lacquers; it may have suggested this form to the lacquer workers of the Kamakura period in Japan.

Before the end of the Heian era most Japanese lacquer designs were symmetrical and ornate and in the stately flowing style of T'ang Dynasty China from which they were obviously borrowed, but at this period the Japanese workers discovered the *maki-e* technique and with its arrival the asymmetrical but balanced designs of purely Japanese taste become dominant; these make use of a few simple objects, such as wheels and waves, with a great power of poetic suggestion. This style did not change until fairly late in the Kamakura era—a rather remarkable phenomenon in a period which saw so many changes of taste in other arts and one which, it has been suggested, may have been caused by the love of lacquer shown by Masako, the wife of the warrior Shōgun Yoritomo. However, later in the period a more austere and sober style prevails, although one

Four-case *Inrō*. *Nashiji* ground with all-over design of chrysanthemums in *togidashi*. Length 3 inches. Width 2½ inches.

which, when fully developed, gives an overall impression of great splendor. In this only one or two materials are used, frequently with burnished gold grounds and with an inlay of one kind of material only.

In the Muromachi period, under the all-pervading influence of Zen Buddhism, the designs used by the lacquerers were much simplified, great use being made of empty space; the objects which are drawn are defined in *maki-e* or *takamaki-e* techniques. These designs were on the basis of the themes used by the Kanō and the Yamato-e style painters and often contain one or more literary allusions. To help the appreciation and identification of these latter, Chinese characters are now used for a part of the design—a custom that was to become very common later on and persisted until modern times.

Lacquer designs in the succeeding Momoyama period made a typical use of *hiramaki-e* and were marked by their strong feeling for a naturalism that had not yet appeared in the history of the art of lacquer. Where in the preceding era a whole scene was typically shown, in the Momoyama only parts of the whole were depicted and these were greatly enlarged and brought to a focus that immediately engages the attention of the onlooker. Often part of the scene or object depicted is cut off by the edges of the box, and this makes for an effect of richly poetic suggestion. This may be heightened by the use of grounds like the "pear-skin" (*nashiji-nuri*) in all its forms and the aventurine texture (*nashi*) of parts of the composition.

Towards the end of the Momoyama period the tempo of the discovery of new techniques greatly speeded up, and in the Edo age the mingled use of these forever new effects still further increased. It is to this epoch, the Edo of the Tokugawas, that more than ninety-nine per cent of the old work found for sale belongs and much of it comes too from the nineteenth century. However, except perhaps for an occasionally over-displayed ingenuity, lacquerwork remained without any trace of decadence and there are still many fine pieces available to the collector almost all of which have, if made before about 1860, a beauty which many enthusiasts believe to be unique in the whole range of art experience. *Inrō* are the most commonly available but there are also a number of fine writing boxes (*suzuri-bako*), document boxes (*bunkō*), boxes for letters (*fu-bako*), for poem cards (*tanzaku-bako*), cabinets for the incense ceremony (*kō-dansu*), charcoal jars (*hitori-kōro*), boxes (*kōgo* and *kō-bako*) of various kinds and, what some may feel most desirable, lacquer objects for the tea ceremony, tea jars (*natsume*) and *cha-ire* and boxes (*cha-bako*), and lastly the often very charming picnic sets (*bento-bako*). Among smaller articles are combs, hair ornaments, *sake* bowls and bottles.

Further Reading

Yoshino, T., *Japanese Lacquer Ware*, Tōkyō, 1959. (A most excellent work by a foremost authority which deals also with modern techniques.)

Strange, E. F., *Catalogue of Japanese Lacquer*, Part 1—General, Part 2—Inrō, H.M.S.O., London, 1924 and 1925.

Japanese Art and Handicraft, Guide to the Exhibition in aid of the Red Cross, London, 1915. (It contains an important section on Lacquer.)

Joly, H. L., *Catalogue of the W. L. Behrens Collection*, Part 2—Lacquer and Inrō, London, 1913.

Tomkinson, M., 'Inrō', *Trans. Proc. Japan Soc.*, vol. 3, sect. 2, pp. 22–33, London, 1895.

TEXTILES

The arts of dyeing and weaving were perfected in very early times in Japan and almost incredible skill was acquired by the Japanese worker using primitive tools and methods that show, over their long history, an evolution more uneven in its pattern and slower in its tempo than that of most other crafts. The results, however, have been fabrics so glorious that Western collectors have vied to obtain them since they first became known in Europe. Good examples still appear for sale but they become rarer each year and the finest are now probably only to be seen in the great national collections of Britain, France and the U.S.A.—some of those in the last-named country being particularly rich in the resplendent robes created for the Nō drama.

Woven materials are known from very ancient times. These in-

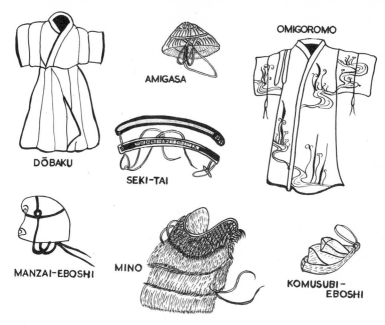

DŌBAKU

AMIGASA

OMIGOROMO

SEKI-TAI

MANZAI-EBOSHI

MINO

KOMUSUBI-
EBOSHI

cluded a striped material (*shitori*)—possibly like the recent *Sanada-himo* used for men's belts—a hemp cloth made from bark and a mulberry cloth. They were dyed probably without patterns by plant extracts. In A.D. 216, a Korean woman weaver named Saiso came to Japan and she seems to have been followed by many Chinese weavers who settled in the country and introduced the weaving of brocades. In the Nara period many kinds of silk brocades were being produced, among which were those with patterns of flowers, wheels, *kiriu*, and lozenge-shaped designs. The motifs for these seem to have been at first mostly copies of the materials used in the T'ang Dynasty times in China, but although the fashion of wearing Chinese brocades and embroideries lasted down into the Heian period, at least among the nobles, it seems that purely Japanese designs were also produced at an early date. Many of the Chinese fabrics of these early centuries can still be seen in the treasury of the Shōsōin at Nara: besides brocades (*nishiki*), they include damasks and silk gauzes and symmetrical plant and animal designs; very grand, powerful and imposing are the typical motifs. In the later Heian era, with its disregard of history and its love of whatever was new and fashionable, its amazingly sophisticated cult of the contemporary, the purely Japanese textile art—Japanese in design and fabrication—came to its full establishment.

After the fall of the Heian culture and the decay of the nobility who had patronized the weavers, many of the old techniques were forgotten; dress became simpler and more practical as befitted the martial temper of the times; the *kosode* (a garment with short hanging sleeves) replaced the elaborate court dresses and the designs that this carried were produced largely by a system of tie-dyeing (*shibori*) which was cheaper and simpler than both the old complicated weavings and the former wax-resist methods that were not very different from the better-known *batik*. However, the long over-garment worn by women (the *uchikake*) was the means of stimulating several new techniques which included both more detailed embroideries and the process known as *surihaku*, which was a means of printing designs of thin gold and silver sheets on to silk. During all this period, however, fabrics of all kinds were imported from China and even from India and these left a rich legacy to the native productions of later ages, showing influences of the art of the Sung, Yuan and Ming times of China and of the cotton prints of India. Some of these ancient fabrics may still be seen as the mounts of famous paintings in the *kakemono* form.

Two new requirements engendered in these centuries stimulated the textile worker to new productions. One of these was the custom of using a square of some fine fabric to wrap around the more precious items of the tea ceremony. Later, this developed into the *fukusa*, a cloth square used for wrapping up presents and later returned to the donor as a kind of token receipt from the recipient of the gift. These *fukusa* are frequently of great beauty, all shades of rose, yellow, green, silvery grey, creamy white and perhaps most beautiful of all, tea-leaf and withered leaf colors for designs that are almost always in impeccable taste and are often of ineffable loveliness. The other product which called on all the resources of the textile arts in the centuries immediately prior to Tokugawa times was the robes used for the *Nō* plays. The designs for these were mostly embroidered on heavy brocade weaves; each kind had its own special name and was reserved for certain roles: as examples

82

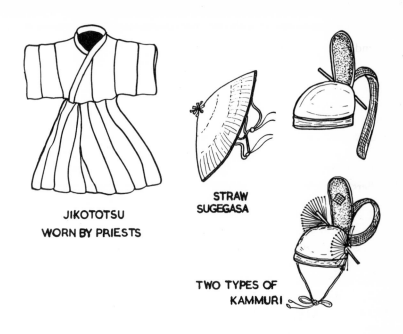

JIKOTOTSU
WORN BY PRIESTS

STRAW
SUGEGASA

TWO TYPES OF
KAMMURI

may be cited the *Kariginu*, properly a hunting cloak, used for male roles exclusively and carrying such designs as double branches of Scotch pine and formalized cloud scrolls (as does one in the collection of the Marquis Moritatsu Hosokawa), carried out in a heavy brocade weave, and contrasting with this, the *Nui-haku*, the designs of which are produced with colored embroidery and gold and silver thread with appliqué of gold leaf. One in the Tōkyō National Museum is of fine woven silk, imprinted with gold leaf and embroidered with designs of flowers and buds and leaves in bright red, old rose, golden yellow, greens, deep blues and a shade which calls to mind that of autumn-tinted maples. Such a robe was always for a female role. Another in the same collection and dating from the Momoyama period is of a russet-brown silk on which is printed wavy bands of gold-leaf; it has embroidered on it wonderfully bold yellow and white lilies with black and yellow leaves and much smaller patterns of *gosho-guruma* (the two-wheeled vehicles used by the court nobles in the Heian era). The whole design calls to the

83

mind the atmosphere of some old romance of the Heian period and yet, like all these Nō robes, it has a boldness well fitted to have its effect on an observer seated at some distance from the actor. This is something of an exception in the whole range of Japanese textiles since, apart from these robes, altar cloths and robes of ceremony used by some priests, all the cloth was used for personal clothing and the rule is that these carry very small designs. In later times, of course, especially in the Edo period, the kind of clothes worn by the different classes was governed by sumptuary laws.

The loom on which such fabrics as these were woven was astoundingly simple. The vertical threads of the warp were stretched between two rollers and from the top of the loom hung two frames or headles which were worked by treadles which raised or lowered them. A shuttle containing a bobbin which held the thread was passed through the alternate warp threads when the first headle raised all the odd-numbered ones and it was thrown back through the warp when the even-numbered warp threads were raised. The accumulating threads of the weft were beaten up together by a batten, both the batten and the shuttle being worked by hand and the headles by the treadle, the warp being kept tight by the action of the rollers. In the weaving of brocades more than two headles were used and sometimes more than one shuttle in which the threads had to be changed from time to time as the pattern demanded. The most complicated floral patterned brocades often required two persons, the weaver working the shuttle and changing the thread and a female assistant working the headles. The late W. Crewdon said, "It is also probable that no other weavers have been able to make use of so many different colored threads. The work done by the shuttles of the Japanese weavers is often more of the nature of darning than weaving."

Many other things besides silken brocades were produced in Japan. Velvet (*birōdo*), thought to have been copied from the velvets given by the Pope to the sixteenth-century Japanese ambassadors, was produced in several varieties, and one frequently finds it in the form of the peculiar cut velvet pictures that were produced in Japan, mainly at Kyōtō, in the last century. Cotton cloth (*momennuno*) was produced in Satsuma about 1550 and soon took the place of the earlier hemp cloth (*nuno*); the weavers of Hizen later made a striped cotton called *Nagasaki momen*. In early times a woolen cloth was manufactured at Shimozuke and later, in Echigo, one made wholly of rabbits' hair, but all fell out of production in the eighteenth century. Damasks (*donsu*), satins (*shusha*), figured silks (*rinzu* and taffeta (*khōaku*) were all being produced before the eighteenth century. Among the weaves produced in Japan and wholly originated in that country is the extremely beautiful silk called *aya*. A heavy silk fabric with oblique lines woven into the pattern, it was produced in several traditional designs such as *saikwa*, rape flowers; *yasō*, wild grass; *rensui*, waves; and *koku*, rice shells, to name but a few. Its manufacture was started in very early times and with rather varying fortunes was produced without a break until quite recent times. Very lovely examples may sometimes be found for sale.

The dyeing of silks by means of resist techniques was developed at least as early as the Heian era. With the partial decline of the more complicated weavings in the Kamakura and Ashikaga times the methods of dyeing evolved rapidly so that by the Momoyama period the most complicated forms of weaving, dyeing, embroidery and hand painting might all be combined with new effects on one fabric. Wax-resist methods and tie-resist methods, the latter in later days having its rough outlines sharpened by painting in, were developed early and used later only sporadically and mostly in provincial centers. But in the late seventeenth century Miyazaki Yuzen, a Buddhist priest and a celebrated *Ukiyo-e* painter, invented the method which became known as *Yuzen*, although there is reason to believe that it was borrowed, in part, from the Dutch. In this, an artist drew the outlines of a design upon silk and the dyer then went over this with a paste made from rice or from buckwheat powder and alum, squirted, in ever-varying amounts to follow the modulations of the original line, from a brass funnel with a paper top that could be held in the hand and have varying pressure applied to it. The areas enclosed by the lines were then filled in with different colors derived from vegetable dyes. When these were dry the resist outlines were removed by steaming and then the whole of the colored portion was covered with the resist. The whole fabric was then dipped to give the ground color desired.

Another very popular method was that of crêpe-printing; this continued into modern times and good examples of it are fairly common. The crêpe fabric, called *chirimen*, was produced by weaving with threads to which a very strong twist had been given and on this a stencil plate (*katagami*) was fixed with bradawls. A resist paste was now spread over the whole, thus blocking in those parts of the design that were to be left white. Different parts of the design were worked out by different stencils and then when dry, were dyed. The delicate paper stencil plates used for this work may still occasionally be found for sale and are beautiful objects in themselves.

Further Reading
Priest, A., *Japanese Costume: an exhibition of Nō robes, etc.*
New York, 1935.
Kawakatzu, K., *Kimono*, Tourist Library, Tōkyō, 1936.
Gunsaulus, H. C., *Japanese Costume*, Boston, 1923.
Crewdon, W., 'The Textiles of Old Japan', *Trans. Proc. Japan Soc.*, vol. XI, pp. 4–23, London, 1912.

SWORD FURNITURE, ARMS AND ARMOR

The arts of armor and the sword were pre-eminently the arts cultivated by the *samurai* and the military nobility (*buke*) and such a society placed the armorer and swordsmith above and beyond all other artists. It is in keeping with the esteem these arts were afforded in feudal Japan that a recent authority (Dr. Asako Matsuoka), writing of the *ōyoroi* armor given by Yoshitsune to the Kasuga shrine in A.D. 1190 and still preserved there, says, "it is the type which competent authorities regard as the choicest artistic heritage of the nation." Although no other nation has ever rivalled the craftsmanship of the Japanese metalworker and although no other metalwork has ever been produced that showed such artistry as the sword fitments of that country, it is unlikely that Westerners appreciate these products in quite the same manner as do the native experts (*mekiki*) whose skill in the judgment of swords is often passed down, in hereditary descent, from generation to generation.

Japanese armor, composed of hundreds of small strips (*kōzane*) of steel, iron and toughened hide strung together with leather or silk, some of the plates quite frequently being lacquered, is still moderately common in Western collections and desirable specimens

Tsuba (sword guard). Herbs of the four seasons: brown iron inlaid with gold. Signed: Fujiwara Kiyonaga of Yamashiro, with a kakihan (written seal). Tanaka School early nineteenth century.

are still among the cheapest of available Japanese art works. Most of it dates from the eighteenth and nineteenth centuries and any armor dating before the sixteenth century is extremely rare. Originally there were two types of armor, the *ōyoroi* (worn by the higher ranks) was a scale armor and comprised the helmet (*kabuto*) often exceedingly ornate; the suit (*yoroi*); shoulder pieces (*ōsode*); a mask (*hatsuburi*) (this piece was especially favored after the fourteenth century when mounted fighting declined); the gorget (*nodowa*); sleeve pieces (*kote*) (which in Japan took the place of a shield, an article never used after the prehistoric period); thigh plates (*hizayoroi*) and greaves (*suneate*). The other type, lighter and much more flexible, was the *haramaki* (belly wrapping) worn by the lower ranks and affording much greater ease of movement although obviously less protection since it had no helmet and lacked the important shoulder pieces of the *ōyoroi*. By the sixteenth century, however, these two important pieces had been added to the *haramaki* and under the tassets (*kusazuri*) it became customary to wear a kind of apron for additional protection to the thighs. At this period the distinguishing sign of rank is to be found primarily in the highly elaborated helmets of the leaders which are almost always decorated with antlers (*kuwagata*), while the common soldier wore only a *jingasa* of lacquered leather.

The two great families of armorers were the Miōchin, who functioned as court armorers down to the eighteenth century, and the Saotome—really a younger branch of the former. The work of these families is noted for both the thinness and strength of the iron plates which they used; one late sixteenth-century helmet by a Miōchin smith, twelve inches by ten by eight inches in height, and of quite incredible strength, weighed only two pounds two ounces.

Kashira. All-over pattern of chrysanthemums in relief. *Sentoku* inlay on *Shakudō.*

Menuki. Dancer in the black mask, *kohushiki.* Black metal (not *shakudō*) inlaid with *sentoku.* Length 1⅛ inches.

Many of these helmets were decorated with intricate *repoussé* work, often in the form of dragons.

By common consent the Japanese sword represents the apogee of the metalworker's art. Its forging was conducted with magico-religious ceremony and the smith wore ceremonial clothes for this similar to those of the nobility. These swords are divided into two classes according to whether or not they were made before 1600: those of the earlier date are called *kotō* (old swords) and the later ones *kinkotō* ("near old") or *shintō*. Even during the long era of peace of the Tokugawas the standard of sword making was consistently high with some falling off in quality only in the first half of the eighteenth century, but at the end of that century there was a great revival of the craft associated with Suishinshi Masahide (1750-1825) similar to the revivals which had been experienced in the seventeenth century when many of the best blades were produced by the swordsmiths of Yedo and Ōsaka. Swords were always

Tsuba (sword guard). Tiger and Dragon: *shibuichi*, chased and inlaid with various metals and alloys, both animals in high relief. Signed: "Shozui, at the age of 72." This is the artist Otsuriuken Masayuki (1695-1769), the founder of the Hamano school.

worn in pairs by the *samurai* although never so by other classes, who were forbidden this privilege by law. In battle the warrior had a long sword (*tachi*) at his left side and a short sword (*tantō*) in his girdle; on civilian occasions and out of armor he wore a long two-handed sword (*katana*) and a shorter personal sword, the so-called "companion sword" or *wakizashi*. It was on the two latter that all the refinements of the decoration of the associated sword furniture were lavished. Sometimes one may see short straight dirks which are without guards; these are called *aikuchi*. In judging swords the characters of the different parts of the blade, as shown in the accompanying diagram, are of great importance, especially the nature of the *yakiba*, the shape of the *bōshi* and the character of the file marks (*yasurime*) on the tang (*nakago*). Indeed it was part of the complicated etiquette that grew up around the handling of the sword that, in making an inspection, the observer, standing near a window and holding the blade vertically, should consider in order the following points: (1) search for flaws (*kizu*), (2) the shape and workmanship (*tsukuri*), (3) the hardened edge (*yakiba*), (4) the file marks on the tang and, lastly (5) the signature (*mei*).

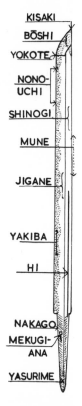

KISAKI
BŌSHI
YOKOTE
NONO-UCHI
SHINOGI
MUNE
JIGANE
YAKIBA
HI
NAKAGO
MEKUGI-ANA
YASURIME

Western collectors, with few exceptions, have always been much more interested in the sword furniture, particularly the guards (*tsuba*) than in the swords and indeed the chiselling and general decoration of these accessories represents an art without equal in the world. Along with the *tsuba* may be considered the *fuchi*, an ornamental band which encircles the hilt at the base; the *habaki*, a metal sleeve, sometimes decorated, on the lower side of the guard;

Menuki. An eagle and a dove, the emblems of Hachiman. Brown *shakudō*. Length 1⅜ inches.

the *kashira,* the cap-like piece placed on the head of the hilt next to the *tsuba;* the *menuki* or ornament—usually a pair—bound on either side of the hilt and formerly serving to cover the *meguki* or pin that held the hilt to the blade; the *kozuka,* a small knife worn at one side of the scabbard—this name was most frequently given to the handle of such a knife which was made to project through one of the holes (*hitsu*—or, if the *tsuba* had two holes, *rio-hitsu*) of the guard; the *kōgai,* a skewer-like implement perhaps derived from the hairpin used with Chinese-style crowns (it exists also in a double form, the *wari-kōgai* or split *kōgai*), the place of which is often taken on swords from Higo province by the *umabari* or "horse needle." All these things are classed as *horimono* or chiselled objects.

The names of nearly four thousand artists have been recorded as concerned with the decoration and design of *tsuba* and *horimono* and these have been divided into schools and families, each with their distinctive character. In later times (seventeenth to nineteenth centuries inclusive) each of these *kinkō* (makers of sword furniture) had at his command a number of processes by which he might produce an incredibly wide range of decorative effects. Iron was the only metal used for the *tsuba* in the fourteenth to sixteenth centuries and was still extensively used but with more decorative treatment, from the seventeenth to the nineteenth centuries. These last three centuries, however, saw the use of softer and more decorative metals and alloys as befitted the peaceful seclusion of the Tokugawas. Silver is sometimes found as an inlay in iron and, more rarely, gold is used for the same purpose. Besides copper, brass, and rather infrequently, bronze, the following native alloys are found: *sentoku*, an alloy of copper, tin, lead and zinc having the appearance of a yellow bronze designed, it is said, to imitate the bronze of the Hsuan Te era (1426-36) of China—when pickled in a solution of copper sulphate it assumes an aventurine sheen; *shakudo*, an alloy made from a base of copper bronze to which from four to six percent of gold was added and which, when boiled in various solutions, turns from red to a beautiful lustrous black—possibly the alloy which has most appeal for the Wsetern collector; *shibuichi*, an alloy of copper and silver, the latter being from a quarter to half by weight of the whole—naturally yellowish, it becomes various shades of dull silvery grey when pickled, but the collector must remember that this delicate patina is frequently destroyed by any kind of organic fat or grease.

Surfaces could be varied by different kinds of grounds being prepared for the design. Of these the following were the most important: *nanako* ("fish roe") a series of raised dots produced by a cupped punch—in work of the highest quality a double or even treble *nanako* ground might be used; *ishime*, a roughened surface tooled with a punch or blunt chisel; *tsuchime*, an *ishime* surface produced with the pane of a hammer; *yasurime*, file marks used for such purposes as the imitation of rain; *amida yasurime* or *amida tagane*, radiating lines made with a file or a chisel; *neko-gake* ("cat scratches") peculiar chisel marks in which the burr is left in place and flattened with a hammer. In addition we find *repoussé* work (*uchidashi*), a term applied to all work that is bossed out from the underside— a type of work common in *menuki*; *mokumé* (the grain of wood), found in two forms, (*a*) that obtained by forging and engraving iron to imitate grained wood, and (*b*) that obtained by soldering and twisting two or more alloys together and then beating them out and cutting them into strips or veneers; *guri-bori*, an imitation of *guri* lacquer made by sweating together thin sheets of *shakudō*, *shibuichi* and sometimes copper and then cutting them into patterns with deep T-shaped grooves—a technique used by a few workers of the Itō and Shōami families.

Of inlays, a common practice in the work of almost all later schools, there are two main kinds, the first, true inlay, or *zogan*, in which metal wires are hammered into grooves and caulked into place and the second *nunome*, or false inlay, in which a thin sheet of metal is hammered on to a prepared surface made of a mesh of chisel cuts, the crossed lines of which make tiny teeth to which the soft metal adheres. A variety of the first exists in the form of the so-called *togidashi zogan*, which is a true inlay of light on dark or *vice versa*, the whole being polished down to a flat surface similar to that of *togidashi* lacquer. When various alloys of different colors are inlaid on iron and their different patinas developed the result is called *iroye* or a colored picture, a technique characteristically used by the Shōami school and others in the eighteenth and nineteenth centuries. Another method of making these colored pictures is by the manner of "brush-stroke" engraving, *katakiri*, much used by such masters as Ōtsuki Mitsuoki in the late eighteenth and early nineteenth centuries. Yet another and commoner form of engraving is *Kebori* (hairlines), minutely fine and incredibly regular incised lines.

The history of sword furniture is an extremely intricate problem and no complete work defining the styles of both schools and individuals yet exists, although good monographs on certain families such as the celebrated Gotō are available. Before the early seventeenth century, almost all guards are of iron worked in simple pierced or chiselled designs or with hammered grounds which show much ingenuity. These for the most part were the work of the armorers. But about the Kwan-ei period (1624-44) when the love of the small, delicate, charming and ingenious began to replace the taste for the ornate, majestic, austere, statuesque and sculptural in so many arts, the sword guard was quickly subjected to the search for new decorative effects and, just as the evolution of sculpture may be said to have finished then, so the evolution of the decorative *tsuba* began.

Below is a short table of some of the main families and schools of the makers of sword furniture, together with the dates they began the making of *tsuba*, etc., and some indication of their styles:

Kaneiye. Fifteenth century. Iron with low relief. Small gold, silver and copper inlay. Subjects mostly those of Chinese Sung and Yuan painting, especially landscape.

Miochin. Fifteenth century. Iron with high relief, sometimes pierced and sometimes with lobed outline; subjects mostly plant forms and animals from dragons to insects.

Umetada. Sixteenth century. Often tough, sonorous iron, but many masters used bronze and a wide range of colored alloys all combined in one work. Flat inlay, details on low relief often in *Kebori*. Some masters use effective *katakiri*. Common subjects plant forms. Mostly signed; after mid-eighteenth century often with plum flower engraved by the character "*tada*" of the name. ("*Ume*" means the plum.)

Goto. Fifteenth century with many branches up to the nineteenth century. Most influential of all schools. Main family of seventeen masters. Used *shakudō*, *nanako* grounds and much gold-zogan. Early ones made only *menuki*, *kozuka* and *kōgai*. In early seventeenth century *shibuichi* used for *tsuba*. From then on issued *orikami* or certificates of origin and authenticity. Designs became rich with much *shakudō* and gold inlay.

Ichinomya. Eighteenth century. Often used *shakudō* with *nanako* ground with inlays of copper gold, grey *shibuichi*. Designs often in low relief. Mostly figures or birds. Other schools derived from Gotō were **Yasui, Kinujo, Kwanjo,** all seventeenth century, and

Ichijo. Nineteenth century. Noted for fine new ground effects often in brown iron or roughened *shakudō* with splendid relief carving.

Nara. Seventeenth century. Wide range of subjects all treated with great realism and using almost all metals and alloys. Some masters use a low, sunken relief. Reliefs in gold and silver often depict birds and flowers; also used subjects from Chinese and Japanese folklore.

Hamano. Early eighteenth century. Low intaglio reliefs, gold *hirazogans*, very high relief and the very finest *keborizogan*, often for fine calligraphy. Splendid new surfaces and patinas. Subjects often from Chinese and Japanese history.

Nomura. Late seventeenth century. Very fine engraving on *shakudō*, *shibuichi*, etc., *nanako* grounds. Flowers and foliage, rarely animals, never humans. *Menuki*, etc., *Tsuba* rare.

Yokoya. Early seventeenth century. A large school with imitators. Noted for *katakiribori* of the very finest quality and fairly extensive use of *shibuichi*. Spirited high reliefs often treated with considerable realism and designs often remind one of those of the *Ukiyo-e* and *Shijō* schools of painters. Many branch schools.

Higo. Seventeenth century. Iron, mostly with black patina and designs in negative silhouette.

Akasaka. Seventeenth century. Iron "open-work" with designs in positive silhouette.

Mito. Eighteenth century. Iron and alloys. Mostly high relief, sometimes within rims. Designs usually contiguous with most of the circumference of *tsuba*. Some inlay but little engraving and almost never *katakiribori*. Often signed "made in Mito." A large school who also copied designs of Yokoya and Nara schools extensively.

Kyoto. Mostly nineteenth century. Used mostly iron with inlay of alloys and gold for faces, etc. Designs mostly taken from Shijō paintings and many of fish, birds, etc.

Yedo. Nineteenth century. Using the immense range of almost all known alloys and metals and specially noted for ornate and detailed inlay. Products appear those of "virtuosi."

The **Hirata** family of Mino (seventeenth to nineteenth century) are noted for decoration of *tsuba* in enamels, often using *tsuba* by other makers.

The foregoing is by no means complete. Several artists worked apart from schools, such as 4 or 5 generations of Kinai of Echizen, whose iron guards are famous for their sculptured dragons. Some worked in several styles and thus copies too often abound, while part of the classification used refers to families and part to towns at which the artists worked. Naturally, all this complicates problems of attribution especially as the Japanese connoisseur looks first at the quality of the engraving while the Westerner is usually pleased first by the inlay.

Among other arms spears (*yari*)—often with beautifully shaped blades and lacquered shafts, glaives (*naginata*), usually with curved blades, and arrow-heads (*yano-ne*) must be mentioned as possessing artistic value. Other pole arms, such as rakes, hooks and barbed T-shaped blades were used only by police and occasionally in sea fights and have little more than ethnographic importance. The arrowheads, which are still easily and cheaply available to Western collectors, include some splendid specimens which would repay further study. They include tripod-shaped types used as fire arrows (*hiyu*) and some beautifully ornate iron votive-arrows designed to be offered at temples. Often these have figures on them and exhortative inscriptions.

Further Reading

Robinson, B. W., *The Arts of the Japanese Sword*, London, 1961.

Hara, S., *Die Meister der Japanischen Schwertzieraten*, 2 vols., Hamburg, 1931–32.

Homma, J., *The Japanese Sword*, Tōkyō, 1948.

Hawkshaw, J. C., and Joly, H. L., *The Hawkshaw Collection of Japanese Sword Mounts*, 1910.

Joly, H. L., *The Naunton Collection of Japanese Sword Fittings*, 1912.

Yumoto, J. M., *The Samurai Sword*, Tōkyō, 1958.

Vautier, P., *Japanische Stichblatter und Schwertzieraten* (Oeder Collection), 1923?

Robinson, B. W., *Arms and Armour of Old Japan*, London, 1951.

Kawaguchi, N., *Kinkō Sōran*, Tōkyō, 1933. (A register of metal-workers in Japanese.)

OTHER METALWORK

Besides the arms and armor the metalworkers engaged in a great number of other productions of almost endless variety: kettles and other articles for the tea ceremony, pipes (in brass for the poorer classes and silver for the wealthier), hairpins, writing utensils especially inkpots and brush-holders, boxes of various kinds and

Sakedzuki (Sake kettle) of cast iron with silver and *shakudō* inlay on the lid. Body decorated with phoenix, dragon and clouds in archaic style.

metal clasps (*kanemono*) in variety, metal beads (*ojime*) attached to the *inrō* and *netsuke*, pouches and purses in chain work and in more recent times vases of great beauty in bronze, iron and silver. Several pouches and metal clasps are known which date from the seventeenth century, but few if any are signed and nothing seems to be known of these workers. One of the most celebrated of the families who made vases, kettles and such was the Komai who were noted for their gold and silver damascene work. Most of the older decorative iron and bronze work, especially that of kettles and lanterns, centered in Kyōto and several studios continued activity there in traditional styles until about 1918.

Among the most beautiful bronze and iron work is that made in earlier times for use in Buddhist temples. Of this class of object gilt bronze is the most common. They include reliquaries (*tō*) of various kinds, such as pagoda-like shapes (*sharitō*), vase-shaped ones (*nōsasshō-tō*), and curious geometrically shaped ones in five layers of monumental form (*gorin-tō*). Flower baskets (*keko*), bowls (beautifully chased examples of these were still made in the modern period), ewers, especially those of elongated ovoid shape with a side spout (*sensan* type), and the pendent gilt-bronze open-work plaques (*keman*) which took the place of floral chaplets behind the heads of statues of divinities, are all objects of intricate and beautiful workmanship, but good examples are very rare in Western collections. More common are the small bronze plaques shaped somewhat like the head of an arrow but broader; these functioned as gongs (*kei*) suspended in wooden frames, and are often, even in late examples, delicately chased. These objects are not usually signed, and since the types often persisted for centuries it is frequently impossible to date them except by the widest approximation.

Bronze and iron articles for secular use are more easily come by and are much more frequently signed and include candlesticks (*shokudai*), incense burners (*koire*), flower vases (*hanaike*) and bowls (*hachi*) to hold miniature gardens. Lastly, there are the bronze and iron *okimono* which are generally signed and often of very fine quality as to metal, patina and casting. These mostly represent animals and those in bronze found in Western collections usually date from about 1760 to 1885. Names occurring on bronzes of this kind, of the highest quality, are Seimin (tortoises), Tōun (dragons), Teijō, Sōmin (animals fashioned after the Shijō painters), Masatsune, Keisai (who also made some fine water pots and brush-holders), Zenrinsai, Gido, Takusai and Hōtokusai. The last four are all nineteenth-century workers.

The iron animals should really be considered in a separate class. These are of two kinds: large models in cast and hammered iron of eagles and dragons (the latter sometimes articulated), and smaller, marvellously articulated models of insects, fish, snakes and crustacea. All of these appear to be the work of the Miōchin school of armorers in the sixteenth and seventeenth centuries (although there seems to be another group, less articulated and usually with brownish lacquered surfaces, which belong to the nineteenth century. The eagles seem mostly to be the work of Munesuke and Muneharu, the dragons of Nobumasa, while among other Miōchin names on the smaller articulated animals are Muneaki, Munemitsu, Muneyoshi and Nobumasa. Some fine falcons and peacocks were made by Sujuki Chōkichi in the late nineteenth century.

Further Reading
Hull-Grundy, A., 'Japanese articulated Animals', *Oriental Art*, new series, vol. 4, No. 4, pp. 144–5.
Brinkley, F., *Japan and China*, 1903—*see* vol. VII.

Pottery and, to a less extent, porcelain are among the least understood of Japanese arts in the West. European works on Japanese pottery are usually defective in detail and in the collections of Western museums there are few fully authenticated pieces, and the more inferior wares have frequently received more than their due amount of attention. It is true that Japanese pottery, more than any other, has influenced the practice of modern potters in the English-speaking world, but this influence is not always fully assimilated and where it is, and where Western design has benefited, it is often solely because wrongly attributed pieces, copies and some forgeries are of underlying sound ceramic concept. Fifty and more years ago salesrooms, like our national collections, abounded in pieces ascribed in happy confidence to the famous potters Tōshirō I and II: now it is known to be extremely doubtful if any piece by either of these potters exists outside of Japan and there are perhaps only some two dozen of their pots even there. There are, too, other difficulties different from those confronting the student of Chinese ceramics; Japanese potteries for the most part have been small family undertakings and of these there are some hundreds that have passed down from generation to generation, each with their own seals or other marks. Sometimes, too, potters who have signed their wares with their own or with one or more art names—different ones at different periods of their lives—have moved from one pottery to another and have often worked in quite different and diverse styles. Only in the last twenty years or so have there been systematic excavations at any of the kiln sites in order to find fragments which will identify wares on other than a literary basis. To all these difficulties may be added the fact that several potteries produced ware only for their local lord—perhaps because lacquer was used for so many things—and this has, of necessity, meant that many wares are little known outside the noble families who still own them or the collections of very rich connoisseurs who have been able to obtain them in recent times.

It must always be remembered, too, that because of the nature of the Japanese house few pieces have been made solely for ornament in Japan; indeed, it is probably true to say that the best pottery of the country has always been made to handle and to use. This is a point to be kept constantly in mind when collecting the pottery and stonewares although, naturally, it applies rather less to the porcelains—a substance for which the Japanese potter has never shown really intimate feeling, although some very fine pieces have been made on occasion.

A native tradition of pottery making goes back to the earliest times and the Yayoi type lasted on in a modified form for some centuries. This style (*hajinoutsuwa*) was replaced between the fifth and sixth centuries by another style imported from the kingdom of Silla (in present Korea) which used a different form of wheel and baked at much higher temperatures in ovens built on hillsides. This ware, with relatively hard fine-grained grey body, is called *suenoutsuwa*. Accidental drops of glaze produced by the chance fall of ash are found on some pieces. In the Nara period green, white, and yellow glazes are found on pots of various kinds, and no doubt some of these were produced in Japan. There is some evidence to show that the finest came from the province of Owari. Probably these were used only for religious purposes, the little that was in domestic use being pieces imported from China. Roof tiles of a brownish green lead glaze are known from the Heian period and

Examples of marks on Japanese pottery and porcelains. 1. Raku. 2. Sen raku yen sei (made at the Senraku garden) on Raku ware. 3. Ōhi. On ware made at Ōhimachi in Kaga since the end of the eighteenth century. 4. Yeiraku. 5. Nippon Yuisetsu. On later Bankō wares. 6. Bankō. 7. Kutani (many variants of this are in use—mostly crudely written). 8. Jiu (Longevity) found on Arita and other porcelains. 9. Dōhachi. Mark of the potter of this name found on Kiyomidzu ware. 10. Kenzan. 11. Ninsei.

Satsuma ware. A dish in *nishiki-yunomi* (brocade cup) style with a decoration of the 500 Rakkan. Hard semi-porcellanous stoneware with vitreous blue-green glaze, the design in both over- and underglaze painting. Made at Nayeshirogawa, Satsuma by Boku Shōkwan, *c.* 1850.

certain glazed temple wares dating from this time are also known but seemingly no real progress in ceramic art was shown and only a few kilns in Bizen, Omi, Iga and Owari continued to produce undistinguished wares for the domestic use of provincials.

In 1225 Kato Shirozayemon (known as Tōshirō) came from China where he had gone to study pottery methods and found suitable clay for his purposes at Seto in Owari. Here he produced the first of a long line of stoneware pots with thick treacly brown glazes in the style of the Chinese *Chien* ware (=*temmoku*) which was much favored for tea drinking in Japan. After Hideyoshi's campaign in Korea at the end of the sixteenth century, many Korean potters settled in Japan. Their products, mostly derived from Korean shapes and covered in greyish-white or cream glazes decorated with designs in brown or blue as well as a grey-green celadon (often with inlaid white decoration) and fawn-colored pottery, stimulated native production. From this sprang many new potteries, of which the most important were those at Kyōto, Hagi, Karatsu, Takatori, and Satsuma. The type of pottery that these produced was very different from the Lungch'uan celadons, Jao-chou, Yao-pien and other Chinese wares that had become so fashionable with aristocrats of the Muromachi time—an era when the native connoisseur developed a true appreciation of the Chinese ceramic triumphs. The change can be seen first at Seto, where Japanese wares copied Chinese shapes but with brownish *temmoku* type glazes already subtly different from the

Vase in Kiōto porcelain; decorated in underglaze green and pale eggplant. Signed: Miyakawa Kozan *c.* 1855.

The god Ebisu on a Tai fish. Bizen ware. Bears the mark of the potter Shimbei (*c.* 1725).

Chinese prototypes. The two great tea masters, Sen no Rikiu and Furuta Oribe also wrought an immense change in the taste of the Japanese *cognoscenti* by their influence. With the rise of the *Wabi* (=rustic simplicity, tranquillity, unpretentiousness) school of the *Cha-no-yu* with its cultivation of *Sabi* the ideals for tea utensils shifted from the Chinese celadons and *temmoku* ware to ones derived from Korean peasant pots with a certain added sophistication. The most important expression of this was *Raku* (=comfort, enjoyment) ware, a soft earthenware, coated with low-toned lustrous glazes fired at low temperatures and so suited to aesthetic amateurs, quick with inspiration but lacking the patience to acquire the more demanding techniques of previous pottery. The first colors used were black and a rare salmon-pink, followed by yellow, cream, green and mixed colors, probably in that order. It was first made at Kyōto by a Korean named Ameya (died 1574) and his son Chōjirō was given a gold seal engraved with the character "*Raku.*" These vessels are thick and frequently purposely crushed to fit the hand after potting. As R. L. Hobson said, "Its essence is that it be made quickly . . . a rapid sketch." Honnami Kōyetsu (1558-1637), a leading amateur expert on almost all the arts, also made *Raku*, but his known work is rare. One famous bowl by him, called the Shōji bowl, has great gaps pulled in the clay (by intention) and filled up with semi-transparent glaze, giving a window-like effect. This was distantly symptomatic of the self-conscious excesses that were to come: lacquered *Raku* such as that made by Haritsu, Miura Kenya and others at Kyōto. *Raku* ware was also made later at Tōkyō, Asakusa, Ōhi, Nagoya, Ōsaka, etc.

Other demands than the tea ceremony were made on the ceramic worker and there finally evolved in Kyōto a cream ware with a hard grey pottery or sometimes stoneware body covered with creamy white or creamy yellow glaze. The manufacture of this spread, in a few years, to other parts of Japan and reached a peak of perfection at Satsuma, where the earliest pieces were decorated in blue and brown underglaze colors like old Korean wares. However, about 1650 Nomura Seisuke (art name Ninsei) learned painting in overglaze enamel from the porcelain makers of Hizen and evolved a truly Japanese style for the first time. He much improved the Awata glaze and painted on it in green, red and brownish-yellow, adding silver and gold, and so brought into being the *nishiki-de* or brocade style. Another potter, Kenzan (1661-1743) who worked at Narutaki (N.W. Kyōto) decorated in underglaze blue and browns, making rought but vital impressionistic sketches of birds, branches and land-scapes first, on his own semi-porcelains and later (?) on the Arita porcelains. His brother Kōrin also tried ceramic decoration—as well as most other things—but although he evolved many most striking designs, sometimes of marvelous decorativeness, closer acquaintance suggests that he did not quite match these to the "ductile fusibility" of clay; in a sense they feel out of character.

Despite some startling and unique successes, the Japanese do not seem, in general, to have been so completely "on terms" with porce-lain as with earthenware. Porcelain materials were brought from China by Gorōdayu go Shōnzui in 1516 and at Arita in Hizen he made a porcelain until supplies ran out. It is decorated in a vivid underglaze blue in the Chinese Ming manner, the themes being birds and blossoms in the style of Kanō painting. Many imitations exist of this and the best are well worth obtaining. After Shōnzui's death (*c*. 1550) a porcelain factory, using native materials, was started at Arita. It was a century later before the making and decoration of this porcelain was perfected and most existing specimens in Western collections date from about 1700 to the present day. Greatest of the potters who worked at Arita was Kakiemon, who perfected color-glaze decoration in Japan. The body of the ware is very variable, grey to white, sometimes crazed and discolored, but with distinguished and elegant designs in soft orange-red, light green, blue, pale yellow, aquamarine, and gold: whatever colors are used there is always plenty of unrelieved white left as a background. Another style (*somenishiki-te*) has designs in underglaze blue cobalt. Almost at the opposite pole of taste to the Kakiemon style is that of Imari; like the Kakiemon stlye, this spread to other potteries and typically is found on a heavy, coarse and rather unattractive paste covered closely with brocade-like designs in a clouded blue and ferruginous red, sometimes with a blackish brown and some gilding. This was imported into Europe in great quantity for nearly two centuries. Most designs of the Edo period ceramics are smaller and more delicate than the bold work of the Momoyama, but this is not always so. Most of the so-called *Kutani* wares made in Kaga province have bold designs, either naturalistic or abstract. Deep red, with green and gold giving an overall matt surface, imposing, rich and refined, this is the so-called *Ko kutani* which was produced from

Examples of potters' marks (mostly impressed). 1. Kimura Shinshiro family on Bizen ware 1700–1760. 2. (with No. 1) Sasude on Oribe ware. 3. Chōju on Oriba ware. 4. Shimbei, on Bizen, Kiōto, Shigaraki and Oribe ware. 5. Moyemon on several different wares. 6. Taihei on Oribe ware and Kaneshige Usuke on Bizen ware 1750–1760. 7. Kōson on Bizen, Kiōto, Oriba, Awata, etc. 8. Manyemon on different wares 1590–1610 and Hirosawa on Bisen 1596-1615. 9. Kimura Rokubei on Bizen, Oribe, etc.

about 1640 to 1700. Another style, *Ao-kutani*, characterized by much use of green enamel with a Prussian blue either on the biscuit or overglaze, was produced down to the nineteenth century at Kaga; about 1830 another style of decoration (*akajikinga*) was introduced by Iida Hachiroemon using the matt Kaga red and designs in gold. At its best this ware is extremely beautiful, but there are many inferior pieces. Finest of all Japanese porcelains are those of Hizen and Nabeshima; the latter particularly may be counted among the great porcelains of the world. The paste of these is of great fineness, snowy-white and with meticulously painted designs of the utmost elegance in underglaze blue, green, purple and red, combining boldness, gaiety and sophisticated elegance with perfect potting. A curiously rustic and provincial porcelain is that of Banko ware made at Kuwana in Ise from 1736 to 1795 by a wealthy amateur, Gonzayemon, who used the art name "Banko" for his seal. Actually he produced many kinds of pottery, stonewares and semi-porcelains besides true porcelain, and copied many styles, including the newly imported Dutch Delft. His porcelains often copy the Ming red and green group, especially those of the reign of Wan-Li. In 1830, the son of a dealer in antiques who had bought Gonzayemon's formulae for colored glazes and his Banko seal started a revival in Banko wares. This man, Mori Yusetsu, introduced the use of interior molds, and it is not surprising therefore to find his ware marked by the use of animal ornament molded in high relief. He also used several colored slips. Yusetsu also copied Chinese models but, his products, in porcelain at least, are more sophisticated than the earlier Banko ware.

No ceramics are more characteristically Japanese than Satsuma ware. There were several pottery centers in this province and it is not easy to distinguish all their wares. That of Nayeshirogawa was set up in 1604. At first the production seems to have been of tea ceremony ware, copying that made at Chōsa and using red and white clays: very rare pieces are said to exist with *underglaze* colored decoration. Porcelain was first made in 1660 but was not successful and throughout the history of Satsuma potteries Arita porcelains seem to have been imported and decorated in the Satsuma styles. The well-known so-called "Satsuma ware" was not made until January 1795 by Kawara Juzayemon, and all the early pieces were small, with restrained use of colored enamels and gold. Previously the products of this pottery had been a grey stoneware with *mishima* decoration (parallel and zigzag stripes) a red stoneware and a black faience. The large, heavily enamelled and gilt bases were first produced in 1872 by Chin Jukwan, who made some very chaste open-work decoration about 1888. The ordinary white ware was sold for decoration in Kagoshima, Tōkyō and Kōbe in the latter half of the nineteenth century.

At Imbe in Bizen are kilns which have operated since the fourteenth century, at first making a red stoneware with a natural glaze and later, after 1583, with a thin "salt" glaze, perhaps in imitation of Chinese I-hing (*boccaro*) ware. At first tea utensils were made in this "*ko-Bizen*" but in the late seventeenth and eighteenth centuries appeared many excellently modelled figures; a number of these pieces have a fine metallic sheen giving the appearance of bronze. In the seventeenth and eighteenth centuries was made a slate-colored ware (*Ao-Bizen*)—an extremely fine and hard stoneware. A white ware is also said to have been produced.

Further Reading

Groves, W. P., 'Some Little-Known Japanese Wares', *Trans. Japan Soc.*, vol. 32, pp. 25–36 (1935).

Franks, A. W., *Japanese Pottery*, London, 1880. (Still useful but must be used with care.)

Hobson, R. L., 'Notes on Japanese Pottery', *Trans. Japan Soc.*, vol. 28, pp. 98–109 (1930).

Mitsuoka, T., *Ceramic Art of Japan*, Tōkyō, 1949.

Okuda, S., et al. Miller, R. A., ed., *Japanese Ceramics*, Tōkyō, 1960.

Hobson, R. L., *A Guide to the Pottery and Porcelain of the Far East*, London, Brit. Mus., 1924. (Japanese pp. 123–57.)

Audesley, G. A., and Bowes, J. L., *Ceramic Art of Japan*, London, 1881. (Still useful as a guide to the later pieces. All earlier dates unacceptable.)

The origins of these are multiple and confused. Printing sacred texts and icons from engraved stones and copper plates was a method of reproduction early practiced in China and Korea and no doubt this was imported into Japan along with Buddhism. Indeed such plates (*bōshimei*) engraved with epitaphs are known from Japan as early as the seventh century. Woodblock printing was later utilized in all these countries, but prayers printed in this way are known from Japan in the eighth century. Since the demand for anything other than religious matter was so small in Japan the printing of books of secular interest came only after many centuries, although illustrated woodblock, printed Buddhist books (*kyō-mon*) are known which date from the early fourteenth century. Side by side with these religious works there existed manuscript novels in scroll form illustrated by *Yamato-e* painters, but they were very rare and restricted in their circulation to a few members of the aristocracy. In the Muromachi, Momoyama and earliest Edo periods, the *Nara-ehon* were produced to meet a rising demand; these were books which combined hand-colored pictures with handwritten texts. The subjects were *otogi-zōshi* (servants' entertainments), *kōwaka-mai* (texts of the *kōwaka*, a dance-like dramatic performance without music) and shortened versions of Heian romances like the *Genji-monogatari*. With the growth of the richer urban merchant and artisan classes in the Edo period it was obviously but a short step to the production of the *ehon*, or illustrated books, which appeared in great numbers throughout Tokugawa times and which, for the most part, were intimately connected with the *Ukiyo-e* color prints.

Another source of the *Ukiyo-e* subject matter and style is to be found in the printed fans which in the early middle ages often showed genre subjects carried out in the *Yamato-e* style and examples are known on which a writer of the twelfth century has chosen to copy out the Buddhist scripture of the *Hokke-kyō*. These printed pictures are not greatly different from the albums of an eighteenth-century artist like Sukenobu. Some writers have pointed, too, to the influence of the *Ōtsu-e*, folk-art paintings of a peculiarly rough kind made by the peasants of the village of Ōtsu; these

109

pictures were in the early seventeenth century still religious but a little later they turned to an ever-increasing output of satirical subjects, mostly at the expense of the ruling classes and the priests. If, to all these sources is added that of the Chinese genre paintings which were being porduced certainly as early as the Sung dynasty, it is easily seen that some artist like Moronobu Kichibei Hishikawa (died *c.* 1694) or a group of such artists might, with the newer, gayer life of the merchant classes in the early Edo period, easily turn the Kanō or Tosa styles, as they had then developed, to depicting the life of the *demi-monde* and the world of the theatre which was becoming so popular. Here was a school of painting that exactly met the newer tastes of the *chōnin* classes and left for them a memento of the fleeting pleasures of the "floating world" (*Ukiyo-e*). A popular song of the day, sung along the banks of the Sumidagawa by idle young men—sons of fathers who were rich traders—said, "In this dreamland of life find your delight in wine. By the time tomorrow comes, this will be among the dear dead days. Who lives for a thousand years?" This was the atmosphere that set the scene for almost the whole *Ukiyo-e* output of both prints and paintings. The great fire of 1657 which swept away all the cultural objects brought from Kyōto and Ōsaka to Edo gave the final impetus to the immense flood of prints that, in ever-increasing volume, was to pour out of the retail shops of Edo until nearly the close of the nineteenth century.

Examples of the seals of the Censors used on prints. 1. "Aratame" (=Examined). 2. "Kiwame" (=Perfect). 3. The "Aratame" seal combined with a date seal, reading "the first month of the year of the Monkey." This is equivalent to the year 1860.

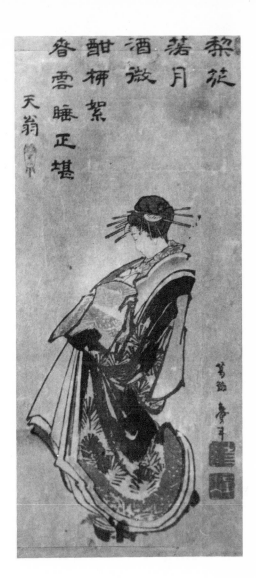

Ukiyo-e Print by
Katsushika Taito (fl.
1825–1853). An Oiran
on parade from the
series *Harimaze Han.*

Realizing that this new demand was far greater than the painters of the *Ukiyo-e* school could supply, the wholesale publishers of printed books (*jihon*) organized the printers, blockcutters and

111

artists into a production group. From 1670 to 1700 there were four such firms of publishers; in 1730 there were thirty and in 1810 forty-seven, rising to fifty-eight in 1840. The publisher is therefore a very important factor in the production of all prints and it is essential that the collector should be able to identify the seals of publishers when they are present on a print, as they usually are. The *surimono*, small prints produced usually with impeccable techniques, using expensive methods and paper and serving the purpose of a kind of greeting card, were often the work of amateurs and do not have publishers' seals; some of them, like some prints, seem to have been designed by amateur comic poets of aesthetic tastes who sometimes commissioned artists to produce prints in conformity with their own desires; the ideas for many earlier prints seem to have come from members of the new *chōnin* intelligentsia.

Various one-sheet prints by Moronobu as well as picture books and story books by this artist appeared on the streets of Edo between 1660 and 1680 and some of these contain an appendix on how to color the prints so that, in some ways, they may also be looked upon as a kind of painting book. In a very short time after the black-and-white illustrations appeared there came into being various kinds of colored print. Possibly the first of these was the *tan-ye*, a picture printed in black and white to which a few pure colors were added by hand; the name comes from the commonest of these colors (*tan*), a kind of orange-red, but occasionally vermilion was used as well. Later came the *beni-e* which was colored by hand with rose madder —often extremely beautiful in those examples in their original condition—and sometimes this, as well as other prints, was heightened in effect by having details such as the eyes of figures put in by hand, using small spots of lacquer or a very lustrous and thick *sumi* ink; these are known as *urushi-ye*. From this it was only a step to the *benizuri-e*, which was predominantly colored by the rose pigment applied by a separate printing block. Later colors such as yellow, blue (which often oxidizes badly and is destroyed) and an extremely charming apple green were added to such prints and then came the full colored print (*nishiki-ye*) in which all the colors are fully printed from separate blocks, being aligned only by small engraved guide lines (*kantō*) which, in the best work, ensures a true registry of the colors. This last simple device is generally supposed to be the invention of the publisher Kishiemon Kamimura, who had the trade name Emiya, and to have been first used in the year 1744. Before this, books in several colors had appeared but these followed the Chinese woodcut practice in dispensing with black outlines so that the registry of the blocks was much more easily accomplished.

The Hishikawa school—the name given to the followers of Moronobu—rank among the Primitives of the Japanese print: their subject matter was, for the most part, the men and women of

"Primitive" Print by Torii Kiyotada (fl. 1714–1745). *Hoso-e* format. *Beni-e:* colored by hand.

their own time, particularly courtesans, the figures often being enlarged to occupy the greater part of the area of the print. Of this school Sugimura Jihei is noted for some rare eortic works of fine design and most of the other followers of Moronobu produced some prints of this kind (*shunga*). The members of the school can, for the most part, be identified by the use of "Moro" as the first syllable of the name but this is not invariable and neither is the subject matter, since legends, historical episodes and even *Kabuki* (the name given to the popular theatre employing live actors as distinct from both the *Nō* and the *Ningyōshibai* or *Bunraku*, i.e. the puppet theatre) scenes all occur, although they take a minor place. In all these prints the surroundings of the figures are usually suggested and these may be emphasized occasionally to rank as true landscape delineation.

It will be seen, therefore, that almost all the themes which are the subject matter of the later prints were already present in work of this early school. The rare Kaigetsudo school produced prints of single courtesans in their beautiful robes, portraying them in great upward swirling brushstrokes. The Torii school founded by Kiyonobu (1664-1729) concentrated on theatrical subjects—although other themes also occupied it—and its prints were probably used as handbills to advertise performances and star performers. At this time also prints began to concern themselves with the new *aragoto* style—a kind of "rough house" or bombastic method of acting—

Devices used by the publishers of color prints. Those shown are the devices of: 1. Yamaguchi-ya Tōbei, found on prints by Utamaro, Toyokuni, Kunisada, Kuniyoshi, etc. 2. Yamamoto-ya Heikichi, found on prints by Hokkei Kiyohiro, Kiyomitsu, Kuniyasu, Kuniyoshi and Gōtotei Kunisada, etc. 3. Yamada-ya Shōhai, found on prints by Kuniyoshi, Toyohiro, Utamaro and Hiroshige, etc.

and from then on multitudes of actor prints of all kinds were to portray these exaggerated gestures. In the same way the print artists recorded for their customers the special poses (*mie*) which some roles called for, these marking some special climax of the drama (*miseba*) into which all the action froze for a short while, the actors often crossing their eyes and holding grimaces as an indication of tensions. Later print artists such as Toyokuni and Kunisada turned out hundreds of such prints to meet the insatiable demands of the theatre-goers of their time.

Pictures of beautiful women (*Bijin-e*), both the denizens of the Yoshiwara as well as tea-house waitresses and others, became a dominant theme and some artists like Kiyonaga and Utamaro specialized in them. A curious method of presentation of such themes was by means of a device called the *mitate* or analogue, by which girls were likened to the hours of the day, to poems, to heroes, to notable scenery or even to posting stations on the main highways, the analogue being sometimes presented in a small reserve in the corner or else by having some object introduced which would call the proper parallel to the mind of the viewer.

Pure *Ukiyo-e* landscape prints came into being with Toyoharu (1735-1814) but we associate with this theme, pre-eminently, the names of Hokusai (1760-1849) and Hiroshige (1797-1858) and their schools. Landscape, birds and flowers and such themes, deriving in part from the Chinese school of Japanese paintings and from Chinese manuals of painting, were the common subject matter of such publishers as Hishiya Magobei of Kyōto and elsewhere, who produced a type of illustrated book either in the styles of the classical schools or in that of the *bunjingwa* (literary man's painting) but in any event outside of the *Ukiyo-e* school which was, for the most part, confined to Edo. Later, however, such artists as Sadanobu, followers of Kunisada and followers of Hokusai produced in Ōsaka a separate school, specializing mostly in theatrical portraits and landscapes and marked by printing techniques of a very high order.

Recent monographs exist on many of the notable artists and new viewpoints and some otherwise rather inaccessible material may be found in the beautifully produced and reasonably priced works by Dr. Lubor Hajek. The works of J. Hillier are also well illustrated and authoritative. Mrs. Brown's book, a mine of information, must be used with care and supplemented by Toda, K., *Descriptive Catalogue of Japanese and Chinese Illustrated Books in the Ryerson Library*, Chicago, 1931.

Further Reading

Binyon, L., and Sexton, J. J., *Japanese Colour Prints*, revised edition, London, 1960.

Strange, E. F., *Japanese Colour Prints*, H.M.S.O., London, 1911.

Ficke, A. D., *Chats on Japanese Prints*, London, 1915, new ed. 1959.

Stewart, B., *On Collecting Japanese Colour Prints*, London, 1917.

Stewart, B., *Japanese Colour Prints and the Subjects they Illustrate*, London, 1920.

Stewart, B., *Subjects Portrayed in Japanese Colour Prints*, London, 1922.

Brown, L. N., *Block Printing and Book Illustration in Japan*, London, 1924.

Hillier, J., *Japanese Masters of the Colour Print*, London, 1954.

Ledoux, L. V., *Japanese Color Prints in the Ledoux Collection*, 5 vols., New York, 1942–51.

Michener, J. A., *The Floating World*, London, 1954. (Contains well-annotated bibliographies.)

Takahashi, S. *The Evolution of Ukiyoe*, Yokohama, 1955.

MISCELLANEOUS ARTS OF MINOR IMPORTANCE

There are several productions of the Japanese which, ranked as a minor art in that country, have never seriously commended themselves to collectors in the West. One such is the simple artistry bestowed upon the gourd, both the various kinds of pumpkin gourd (*Cucurbita* sps.) known in Japan as *Tōnasu*, *Bōbura* and *Kabocha* and the white gourd (*Benincasia certifera* S.) (Jap. *Tōgan*). These are turned into *sake* flasks called *hyōtan* by excavating the pulp, allowing the outer rind to dry hard and fitting the opening with an ivory stopper. With constant use, these change to beautiful shades of reddish brown, and in earlier times the flasks were fastened to the *Obi* with a cord made of twisted silk and metal, tied in various intricate knots which are an intrinsic part of the whole art. Small gourds were used in earlier times as amulets against sickness and stumbling and these were similarly treated. The most famous collection of these *hyōtan* was that of Dr. Makukata, who owned over 3,500 examples.

The artistic carving and working of bamboo has formed one of the major arts of China, probably from Sung times and certainly from the Ming period, and although the notable carvers and workers of this material in Japan have not been so well documented as in China, yet finely-wrought objects in this material have always been accorded a high place in the country's art. Flower vases (*hanaike*) of many shapes were made of bamboo and used for the tea ceremony as were many of the utensils of the ceremony itself, and all such are highly prized. *Netsuke* were sometimes made of this material as, more rarely, were *inrō*, and some much valued tobacco boxes (*tabako-ire*) are to be found, ingeniously wrought from the root of the bamboo. The finest carving was usually reserved for the brush-holder (*fude-tate*) but, unlike the practice in China, this seems but rarely to have been signed. One of the most notable of carvers of bamboo in the nineteenth century was Kōyama Hikonori, who most commonly carved *hanaike* and *fude-tate*. Bamboos are important, too, in the making of flutes (*fuye*), especially the kinds called *ōteki*, *nokan* and *shinobuye* (it must be noted that the flutes with which herd boys are usually shown in paintings were called *kusakari-bue* and are not in this category) and these are sometimes art works in themselves, being beautifully shaped and proportioned and finished with lacquered thread; the best old ones were kept in finely lac-quered boxes. Objects of plaited bamboo are really to be considered as folk art. Large baskets (*kego*) made for flowers used in Buddhist ceremonies are very ancient.

Glassworking goes back to very ancient times (middle Yayoi) when both glass bracelets and beads (*magatama*) are known; these were apparently made from imported Chinese sheet glass. Both Persian and Chinese objects in glass are known to have found their way to Japan in early times and some are preserved at Nara. Very little indeed is known of the glass of the Heian and Kamakura periods.

and there is no evidence that any pieces of artistic importance were produced. In the Momoyama era Venetian glass was imported and provided a stimulus to native work as did the Dutch glass brought in early in the Edo period. Centers of production existed at Nagasaki (seventeenth century) and Ōsaka (eighteenth century) and some few rare *ojime* beads seem to be still in existence from that period, but very little else. In the early nineteenth century, Edo started production of glassware and some extremely fine cut-glass bowls of the style called *Edo-kiriko* are known but are very rare. The finest glassware is said to have been produced in the province of Satsuma in the first half of the nineteenth century but it was only a few years in production and it is doubtful if any of these *Satsuma-kiriko* pieces have come to Europe.

Although enamelling was an art practiced as early as the Yuan dynasty in China, it did not become acceptable to the Japanese until much later. Translucent enamels were used by Hirata Dōnin and his followers on sword-guards in the seventeenth century, but the processes of cloisonné enamels seem to have been kept secret until Kaji Tsunekichi of Nagoya taught the cloisonné technique in several provinces about 1840. Momonoi Gisaburo set about the systematic production of this ware in Tōkyō in 1873 and a little before this Namikawa Yasuyuki of Kyōto started a school of enamellers there which depended on a highly finished technique rather than bright colored effects and used involved arabesques, diapers and scroll patterns as decorative motifs. The researches of the German scientist Dr. Wagner for the Japanese Government helped this craft; eventually Sosuke Namikawa invented cloisonless enamels (*musen*) and Seishi Namikawa brought this technique to a perfection not found elsewhere. The Nagoya school introduced relief cloisonné (*moriage*) and "bodiless" cloisonné (*mutai*) and the best of these works, although late productions and usually expensive, are extremely fine.

NOTES ON SOME MATERIALS AND METHODS USED IN JAPANESE ART

Paper. Said to have been introduced into Japan in A.D. 610. In early papers the bark of the *kōzo* tree was used. It was boiled with lye of wood ash and a vegetable glue added. Papermaking was for centuries a kind of "cottage" industry and was a common kind of tribute in which taxes were paid. Both *kōzo* and *gampi* were made as early as the Nara period when there were red, blue, indigo, yellow and green papers: these were mostly used for copying sutras. In Heian times light and dark grey paper was made from old and used papers and often old letters of loved ones were remade and Buddhist texts copied on them. A dark blue paper was used for writing on in silver and gold dust, especially for Buddhist texts: this continued to be used for centuries for some religious prints. In Tempyō times much paper was imported from China and Korea. In the Kamakura period papers such as the *torinoko* (very thick, made in Hitachi), *senka* (also thick, used for sutra copying and made in Iyo) and *shuzenji-gami* (made in Izu) were manufactured from *gampi*. This last was especially favored by the Tokugawas from the time of Ieyasu: it had a very light red tint and showed horizontal markings. *Sugihara* paper, white, soft and extremely pliable as well as cheap, was used by *samurai*. *Torinoko* paper of feudal times was made of *gampi* and usually contained clay, which gave it a yellow-white color. *Hōshō* paper, used from the Muromachi period on, was made in Echizen. It is made entirely of *kōzo* and was the paper used for the *Ukiyo-e* prints, but in the eighteenth century it was made in several provinces. *Minogami* paper was used for most old printed books and the sizes of this paper set the standard sizes of books. *Hanshi* papers of all but one variety were made from *kōzo* and are characterized by withstanding very prolonged immersion in water without disintegration. They were used for diaries, journals and ledgers. *Suruga-hanshi*, made from *mitsumata*, was a brown paper of somber tone and great toughness manufactured between 1781 and 1788. *Shifu* was made in Miyagi of two kinds; one with silk warp and paper woof, the other all paper. The first was used for ordinary clothes, the latter for ceremonial clothes and book covers. Leather papers (*kami-gawa*) were very thick and tough and figured in raised floral and other patterns and were used for lining boxes, cases, small chests, etc. *Chirimen-gami* (crêpe papers) were made from old *kōzo* papers, reboiled and colored with persimmon juice (*shibu*). *Suminagashi* (colored figured papers) were in use from the eleventh century to modern times. Originally the figuring was only in the top right-hand corner: this was used for writing *tanka* poems (thirty-one syllables); all were *torinoko* papers of *gampi* dyed with red and indigo. Plants yielding paper are: GAMPI (*Wikstroemia canescens* Meis.), short fibers with dull satin finish.

119

Expensive papers of dignified appearance. Most modern *gampi* papers show close horizontal lines about one millimetre apart and vertical lines about two millimetres apart. It is an exceptionally fine, thin tough paper. KŌZO (*Broussonetia papyrifera* Vent., "paper mulberry") is a long-fibred paper made from the inner bark. These papers have been well described as "masculine and strong." MITSUMATA (*Edgworthia papyrifera* S. and L.) is thin, short-fibred paper, very soft but not exceptionally pliable. Described as "gentle and elegant," it has tiny, micaceous flecks to be seen under a ×10 lens.

Horn. The horns (*tsuno*) of some animals were used to imitate tortoiseshell by etching them. The "horn" of the rhinoceros (*sai*) was much less frequently used in Japan than in China. Japanese sometimes carved and lacquered it. True rhinoceros horn told under microscope by many minute cylinders each with separate center. On polarizing, these have fishscale-like structure, each with a cross.

Mother-of-Pearl. Used mostly in lacquerwork but also sometimes by itself or in other inlay. Known as *Ao-gai*, there are several varieties: *Awabi* (*Haliotis gigantea*) gives iridescence predominantly green with purple; that of *Haliotis diversicolor* Reeve has deeper and redder color, but occurs only in much smaller sheets. Another with much richer, deeper and bluer colors comes from *Nautilus pompilius* Linn., formerly imported from the Ryukyu Islands and used in thin strips. Another form, *saza-e* (*Turbo cornutus* Sol.) yields a fine thick mother-of-pearl mostly red and green in reflection. An under layer of silver foil is sometimes used to bring out the color of very fine, thin sheets of the mother-of-pearl.

Rock Crystal (*Sui-shō*). No hollow-ground vessels of this substance were ever made in Japan. Clear balls (*sui-shōrin*) were made in small size; also beads for rosaries, dice, toggles and buttons of various kinds and, in earlier times, the peculiar geometrically shaped reliquaries (*gorintō*). Sometimes small pieces with grass-green dendritic inclusions of chrysolite (*kusa-iri-sui-shō*) are found.

Amethyst (*murasaki-sui-shō*). Very little used. A few small animal carvings have been seen but are probably of late date.

Agate (*meno-seki*). A small amount of this stone is polished in Echiu and Idzumo but appears to have been used only locally. Polished with garnet sand.

Soapstone (*Rō-seki*). Both greyish white and colored found in Bizen and very seldom used in later times for small carvings. For seals the Chinese agalmatolite or pagodite (*tō-rōseki*) was imported and some extremely fine carving was done by the Japanese in this form, much of which passes as Chinese.

Marble (*sarusa-ishi*). Little used for sculpture except in modern times when the pure white stone of Hitachi was chiselled. The variegated marble of Akasaka was in demand as an inkstone and old ones are collected by a few native connoisseurs.

Slate. Fine old contorted and weathered slates (*seki-ban*) are much in demand for garden features and small bridges, especially where the quality of "*sabi*" is aimed at. The old grey-blue slate (*Amabata-ishi*) found near the little town of that name in Kishiu is highly valued as inkstones (*sudzuri*): a hollow formed one end of a small slip, the whole rubbed and polished, then a coat of Chinese ink given followed by another of tallow (*rō*).

Ivory (*Zōge*). Material to be distinguished by marks like that of the "engine-turning" on metal. Elephant ivory of two varieties: (*a*) "Hard," mostly African; more translucent, warmer in color, less grain and mottling, (*b*) "Soft," mostly Asiatic; more open texture, denser white but sooner turns yellow. Some African ivory seems to have been used in Japan, shipped via India, but little until after about 1880. Hard ivory was used but came from Siam. Sumatran ivory was considered best and like that from Annam was a "short tusk" ivory and solid farther from the tip. Japanese workers believed best ivory to yield a reddish powder when sawn. Some *okimono* in fine African ivory of beautiful translucency and without grain. Hippopotamus ivory used in Japan; color "curdled, mottled or damasked"; denser than elephant ivory. Hard, porcellanous rind removed by repeated heating and cooling, and this sometimes induces "shakes" or cracks. Walrus ivory much less dense than hippo. Oval in section with the cavity extending far up and so leaving only a little solid ivory at the tip. Usually a fine white color, very pure. Large pieces only found in earlier work. "Marine ivory," i.e. narwhal tusk, spirally grooved and usually a waxy golden yellow also used. Fossil ivory (odontolite) found in mammoth ivory where it is converted to a blue substance like pale lapis lazuli. This was very occasionally used in Japanese art. A technique called *Bachiru* known from late tenth century consisted of staining ivory from inside (if hollow) or underside (if flat) and then carving through to the stained parts. Other teeth sometimes used.

Bone (*hone*). This substance used for small carvings; thigh bones or shank bones only chosen and these usually of small size. Cavity of bone marrow unsightly and difficult to avoid. Usually the hollow interior was simply plugged at the ends. A few bones will take a high polish but this is a long process and was seldom expended on such inferior material. Ox and horse bone were mostly used.

Antler. This substance, properly "buckshorn," came only from the male Sika deer (*Sika nippon nippon* Temm.). It was much used by the Asakusa school of *netsuke* carvers. Texture varies according to age of animal, season, whether shed or from dead deer, etc. Generally close texture, denser than most bone, good white but not translucent, sometimes with microscopic dark lines, and occasionally the whole is a dark yellow-brown with a flecked appearance. Interior of the bone has a cancellated structure.

Umoregi. (Sometimes called *Jin-daiboku.*) It is a fossil wood which has become a dark heavy brown lignite. Looks something like dark walnut. Used for some *netsuke* and for small trays, etc., sometimes with applied lacquer designs. It comes from Sendai. The darkest varieties are usually most brittle.

Umimatsu. A substance produced from the corallines of species of *Sertularia* and found on the coast of Oki. A dark brown substance of somewhat horny consistency and often with white spots and streaks or these of paler brown. Pitted and sometimes nodular exteriorly. Used sometimes for *netsuke* and other small carvings.

Tortoiseshell (*bekkō*). Rich yellow-gold, translucent and glowing, this comes from the Loggerhead turtle (*Chelonia imbricata* Linn.). Earlier work was in material imported from China, but a finer quality came in later nineteenth century from London. Plates welded together by heat. Heated material molded in wooden molds. Used for *netsuke* and women's forked hairpins (*kanzashi*): also lacquered over and embedded in lacquer. Panels of this in lacquerwork sometimes have designs in gold drawn on them.

Shagreen (*Same-gawa*). Derived from skin of species of ray (*Rhinobatus sp.*). Imported from south China. Its chief use was as the basis of the shark-skin lacquer "*same-gawanuri*" which was traditionally used to cover the finer scabbards of swords (*saya*).

Nuts. These were sometimes carved to serve as *netsuke* and as beads, especially for rosaries. Perhaps the commonest was the walnut (*kurumi*) (*Juglans Sieboldiana* Maxim.) but the small elliptical acorn-like nuts of *Nelumbium nucifera* Gaertn., known as *hasu-no-mi*, are also used. Vegetable ivory derived from the Corozo and Cohune nuts (*Phytelephas sps.* and *Attalea sps.*) was also used on occasion, but was imported from South and Central America by Europeans. It is very hard, pure dull white and without the grain or markings of animal ivory. The *bin-rōji*, betel nut (*Areca catechu* L.) was also carved.

Woods. Very widely used for building, lacquering, carving, turnery, etc. Following noteworthy: *keaki* (*Zelkova serrata* Thunb.), fine grain, gold brown, annual rings clear, medullary rays fine, pores single, large and open in spring wood, very small, scattered in autumnal wood. Dry weight per cu. ft. 39 lb. 9 oz. *Kaki* (*Diospyros kaki* Linn.), black with streaks of orange, greyish-brown and dull salmon color. Cold as marble. Scent disagreeable. Weight 48 lb. 10 oz. Pores, fine, scarce and plugged; med. rays irregular. Important buildings and all ornamental work. *Tsuge* Box (*Buxus japonica*), deep yellow, fine, dense, surface lustrous, rings obvious, pores larger than European box, weight 73 lb. Used for best wood engraving (some *surimono* appear to have been engraved on this), small carving and turnery. All other wood engraving was done on cherry wood (*sakura*), a close, uniform, red wood. *Hinoki* Cypress (*Chamaecyparis obtusa*), pale straw yellow, lustrous, darker wavy streak, and the whole grain may be exceedingly waved and contorted, annual rings distinct and usually marked with dark alternating belts which are narrow; medulary rays obscure, weight 22-28 lb. One of the most widely used and highly regarded native woods. Korean pine (*Chosen-matsu*) *Pinus koraiensis* S. and Z., like Canadian yellow pine but more reddish and of obviously shorter grain, weight 24 lb. 1 oz. *Isu* wood comes from a kind of witch-hazel (*Distylium racemosum* S. and Z.), the bark used for the glaze of Arita porcelain, when reduced to ash, the wood very heavy and fine-grained and extremely durable, light to dark chocolate-brown, sometimes reddish, with multitudinous minute pores but annual rings and medullary rays indistinct. Used for combs, ornamental turnery and for *netsuke* by Miwa school. Ebony, *kokutan*, various species of *Diospyros* fairly commonly used, usually alternating bands of light brown and black weight 61 lb., all imported into Japan. *Kiri* (*Paulownia imperialis*), extremely light (20 lb.), one of the most prized of all woods. Very light nut red-brown, often with silver-violet luster. Large pores in spring wood all plugged, other pores very small, as are rays. Probably most costly of all woods. Maple wood of two kinds: (*a*) *Momiji* (*Acer palmatum* Thunb.), white to grey-brown, minute pores, weak medullary rays, fairly distinct annual rings; (*b*) *Kaede* (*Acer japonicum* Thunb. and *A. micranthum* S. and Z., and other *Acer* sps.), light pink, very fine grain, minute medullary rays which show as spots in longitudinal section. Surface more lustrous and shiny than *momiji*.

Silk. Several species of silk moth were raised in Japan but only two were used at all extensively, *Bombyx mori* Linn., the true silk moth and the main source of supply, and the Japanese Oak Spinner, *Antheraea yamamai* G. M. The last seems never to have been used by itself. Main kinds of silk are: (1) *Habutae*, ribbed, white, plain and very thick: one thin thread of two strands is wound round a thicker of six strands; (2) *Chirimen*, crêpe, rough and without luster —*Mon-chirimen*, with a raised pattern on a dull crêpe ground— *Yama-ma-ino-chirimen*, with oak-spinner threads mixed with others; the latter take up the dye, the former reject it and so add luster.— *Chima-chirimen*, with *yama-mai*, a striped silk, usually yellow-green; (3) *Kanoko-shibori*, a very light wrinkled silk used as hair ornament or neck band, red or violet with white spots; (4) *Nishiki*, a brocade of several kinds, e.g. *ito-nishiki* gold thread brocade and *aya-nishiki* silk damask brocade which usually has a woven pattern of flowers. The gold thread is made by using lacquer to stick gold leaf to a *Gampi* or *Kōzo* paper cut into thin strips. Several cheaper substitutes are used for less valuable *ito-nishiki*, e.g. tin and silver foil coated with yellow of various kinds.

PART THREE

The subject matter of the arts

Sources for the subject matter of Japanese art

Perhaps no art in the world has a richer or more involved and intricate content than the art of Japan. Motifs from at least two prehistoric cultures lasted down through later centuries and for the most part make up the core of indigenous or native subject matter. The contacts which followed from the introduction of Buddhism and their effects have been indicated in Part One, as have those which were made with the Western world. Buddhism itself brought in its wake Persian and Indian motifs, shapes and suggestions, as well as others from Tibet (especially those connected with the Tantric tradition); in the course of time many hundreds of themes from purely Chinese and, to a lesser extent, Korean sources were imported into the country; some remained to be represented in their original form, others changed to conform to Japanese taste and outlook and still others were dropped after a few years when the current fashion for some aspect of Chinese culture had passed. In theory, therefore, any pictorial aspect of Chinese culture evolved over some four thousand years may be expected to occur, intermingled with those of all other foreign influences, together with those of the whole of Japanese history, myth, folklore, magic and legend, together with (and this is particularly true of the color prints) ephemeral manners, customs and bits of social scandal that were the talk of the Yoshiwara and the world of Kabuki for a week or two. Fortunately for the collector, the matter is, in practice, not *quite* so complicated.

Natural objects

The Chinese and Japanese have always cultivated a taste for peculiar shaped stones and used them particularly in the "flat" gardens. They were classified and named and appear as motifs on lacquer, pottery design, and in some paintings. Plants are first to be grouped approximately in relation to the four seasons of the lunar calendar: 1st month (February) Pine (*Matsu*), 2nd Plum (*Ume*), 3rd Cherry (*Sakura*), 4th Wistaria (*fuji*), 5th Iris (*shōbu*), 6th Tree Peony (*botan*), 7th Lespedeza (*hagi*), 8th a tall grass, *Eulalia japonica* (*susuki*—but the flower is called *obana*), 9th Chrysanthemum (*kiku*), 10th Maple (*momiji* or *kaede*), 11th Willow (*yanagi*), 12th the *Paulownia imperialis* (*kiku*). In more recent times, in the Edo and Meiji periods, other flowers represented the seasons. For example in spring the daffodil (*suisen*) and the crocus-like *Adonis amuraiensis* (*fuku-ju-sō*), really a sort of buttercup; in summer the herbaceous peony (*shaku-yaku*) and the lily (*yuri*), in autumn the lotus (*hasu*), and in winter the crimson plum (*kan-kōbai*). Possibly with reference to ancient Chinese poetical beliefs certain birds and flowers are always associated; so we find the swallow and willow, the sparrow and bamboo, the dove and the plum, the squirrel and the vine, the phoenix (*hō-ō*) and the *kiri* and the quail and the millet; probably to be attributed to native sources are the orange (*tachibana*) and "cuckoo" (*hototogisu*) and the plum and the nightingale (*uguisu*). Often used decoratively is the group known as "The Seven Herbs of Autumn" (*nanakusa*); these are the *hagi*, *susuki*, *kusa* (*Pueraria* sps.) a leguminous plant with purple blossoms, *nadeshiko*, a kind of wild pink, *ominaeshi* (*Patrina* sp.) a yellow flowered valerian, *fujibakama* (*Eupatorium chinense*) a hemp-agrimony with pink and white flowers, and the *asagao* or "Morning Glory" convolvulus, which last is sometimes replaced by the *kikyō* or Bell Flower (*Platycodon grandiflorum*). The Pine, Bamboo and Plum, known as "the three friends" (*Shō-chiku-bai*), are often shown together and are symbolic of longevity, rectitude and sweetness; together they are emblematic of happiness and good fortune. Other plants found in art are the radish (*daikon*) associated with the god Daikoku, the *yamabuki* or yellow "rose" emblematic of money and associated with the legend of Ota Dōkan, the bean (*mame*), emblematic of health and strength, the agaric fungus (*kinoko*), symbol of long life, the seaweed (*kombu*), a New Year symbol of joy, and the fern (*shida*), another New Year symbol, its fronds being attached to the straw rope (*shimenawa*) hung above the *kamidana*.

Animals are even more numerous than plants. The Dragon

126

(*tatsu* or *riō*) is shown as an ornament on almost every kind of work; frequently it is shown in storm clouds around Fuji and is then an emblem of a successful career. The Tiger (*tora*) is often shown with bamboos in a storm which will destroy it, whereas the bamboo survives because it bends. Both Dragon and Tiger appear with various figures representing dozens of legends. The *kirin*, a kind of unicorn, is a paragon of virtue: the *shishi* is something between a lion and a dog and is to be found in pairs to exclude evil, or singly with a ball, the *tama*, jewel of omniscience, and often with a peony, i.e. the king of beasts and the queen of flowers. The twelve zodiacal signs used in denoting years and hours are represented by animals, and sometimes the inclusion of one or other of these in a design may help to date an object or help to identify its subject matter. They are, in order, the tiger, hare (*usagi*), dragon (*tatsu*), snake (*mi*), horse (*uma*), sheep or goat (*hitsuji*), monkey (*saru*), cock (*tori*), dog (*inu*), boar (*i*), rat (*nezumi*) and ox (*ushi*)—the latter is often shown with the herd boy and is then one of the Buddhist "oxherding pictures." Among other animals found in art are deer (stag), either with maple trees emblematic of autumn, in the mountains denoting one of "The 100 poems told by the nurse," or with an old man, the god Jurōjin. Partly real and partly supernatural are the tortoise (*minogame*), symbol of strength and longevity, and the phoenix (*hō-ō*), a portent of good fortune in the near future. Japanese art also uses many sea creatures such as the octopus and clam for decoration.

Legend and folklore

Of the multitude of themes that could conceivably come under this heading perhaps the commonest is that of the *Shichi Fukujin*, the seven Gods of Good Fortune. Most often found of these is the fat, jolly Hotei, the god of contentment, always shown with his bag and sometimes playing with children; Bishamon, a warrior holding a spear and a pagoda, is the god of prosperity; Benten or Benzaiten, a female deity, often rides a dragon or serpent; she resembles Kwannon and is the goddess of beauty, offspring, love and eloquence and, some say, music; Fukurokujin, who has a domed forehead, is a god of longevity and is shown with its symbols, usually a spotted deer, a crane, or a tortoise, or else holding a staff or a peach; often indistinguishable from the last is Jurōjin, god of scholastic success, who

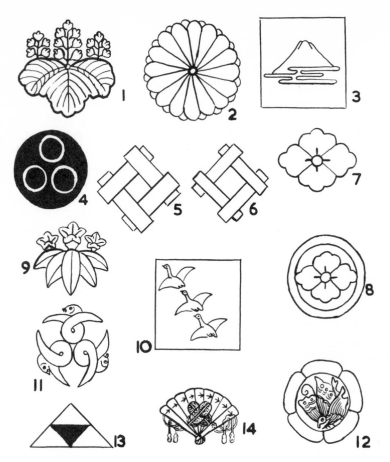

Examples of Mons chosen to show motifs in the formation of these devices, the relationships between some themes and the families that own them and the methods of varying the device. It is a general rule that the larger the Mon the less important the bearer. 1. The 5 and 7 blossom Paulownia crest of the Mikado. Some important Daimyō also used this crest and others those with varying numbers of blossoms. 2. The 16 petal *Kiku* chrysanthemum crest. 3. Crest of Aoki, Daimyō of Asada in Settsu. 4. Matsura, Daimyō of Hirado in Hizen. 5. Sakai, Daimyō of Ohama in Wakasa. 6. Sakai, Daimyō of Matsuyama in Awa. 7. Nambu, Daimyō of Morioka in Mutsu. 8. Goto, Daimyō of Fukue in Hizen. 9. Crest of Fudjioji, Azano and other Kuge families. 10. Crest of Iio, a family of Samurai. 11. Crest of the Daimyō family of Hanabusa. 12. Crest of Ikeda, Daimyō of Katori in Inaba. 13. Crest of the Hojō family. 14. Crest of Akita, Daimyō of Mihara in Mutsu.

may have a white deer, a peach, a staff with a dragon head, or one from which hang books; Daikoku, god of wealth and patron of merchants, is shown as a prosperous old man with rice bales and a mallet, and sometimes a rat nibbles his ear or a hole in his bag; Ebisu, son of the last and god of daily food, has a little beard and is usually a squat, jovial figure accompanied by a great *Tai* fish on which he may ride. Sometimes a second female, Kichijōten, sister of Bishamon, takes the place of Jurōjin and there are other variants. Sometimes these seven gods are shown all together in the treasure ship (*Takarabune*) which has a single sail and is also laden with treasures: it is mostly associated with the New Year. These gods are never shown together before the mid-seventeenth century and as a group they are a comparatively late invention.

Other legendary figures are Daruma, the reputed founder of the Zen sect, who was so long in contemplation his legs withered away, in which state he is shown as a snowman, a children's toy, or as the subject of comical carvings and drawings in which, too, he is often depicted yawning and stretching or being mimicked by an unprepossessing coolie or servant maid. Serious works show him not infrequently crossing the sea on a leaf which commemorates his journey from India to China. A favorite theme is that of one or other of the *rishi* or *sennin* who, by ascetic practices, have obtained immortality and wander in the mountains. Their number is legion, but the commonest in art are: Gama Sennin, with a toad; Kanzan, a stunted form who looks like a madman, expounding a scroll to Jittoku, whose face is furrowed with age; Choryō, shown by a bridge getting a shoe from the river or threatening a dragon; and Tōbōsaku, a smiling old man who either rides on a stag or on clouds, carrying either a leafy branch over his shoulder, or a peach, and is sometimes accompanied by a bat or by Seiōbo, the "fairy Mother of the West"; last, Chōkwarō, who is always shown with a gourd in which is kept his magic folding horse or mule. A Buddhist counterpart to these predominantly Taoist figures are the Rakkan or immediate disciples of Gautama Buddha. Originally 1200, they are more frequently reduced to 500, but for artistic purposes they were grouped as eighteen, which the Japanese reduced further to sixteen. Each of these is identified by his own special attributes and perhaps most common and typical of the group is Kiyataka Tashu

Sonju who is shown as an old man seated on a rock by the sea holding tablets and a short fly-whisk. Also Buddhist are the Tennin, who are similar to the Christian angels and are usually represented as beautiful spiritualized females with phoenix wings, sometimes carrying musical instruments, whose tenuous draperies float in the blue of heaven.

Illustrations of purely Japanese legends are frequently found as the subject matter of art. Among the most popular are those of Urashima and Momotarō. Urashima is the Japanese Rip van Winkle. He catches a tortoise which turns into a princess and lives with her under the sea. After what seem to be three years he returns to earth where, finding everything altered, he incautiously opens a casket the princess had given him. He immediately ages and falls dead. Momotarō tells of an old couple who find a baby inside a peach; when the child grows up he journeys to the land of ogres with his friends, an ape, a dog and a pheasant, and with their help captures the ogres' castle and their treasure. Another frequent subject is Rōsei who, in a dream, lives out a whole lifetime in which he passes from poverty to riches and honor and becomes Emperor, all in the space of time necessary to cook the millet for his evening meal, and this way comes to realize the transitory nature of life and its essential unreality. Other curious legends often depicted on art objects are those of the badger tea kettle which a monk gave to a travelling showman, who made a fortune exhibiting it and ultimately gave it to the temple of Morinji where it was ever afterwards venerated—a subject known as Bambuku Chagama, or the Wonderful Tea Kettle; the giant monk Benkei, who is shown either fighting with the historical hero Yoshitsune, whose devoted servant he afterwards became (cf. Little John and Robin Hood), or with the great bell of Miidera on his shoulder which, having stolen, he afterwards returned for the payment of a vast cauldron of bean soup: finally stories of the monk Anchin, who was destroyed inside the bell of Dōjōji where he had taken refuge from the girl Kiyohime, whose unrequited passion for him had turned her into a demon. She is shown with a snake-like tail wound round the bell heating it to white heat and incinerating thus both Anchin and herself.

Of the many mythical creatures who have haunted the Japanese imagination the most often found are the Tenga and Ashinaga, rather feeble folk, the first with very long arms and the second with long legs, frequently shown helping one another to fish. Rather less frequent as the subject matter of art are the Long Necks and the Vampire Women. The Tengu, creatures with wings, beaks and claws and human bodies, are more often seen. These are a kind of non-malevolent demon, either with human forms but with long noses and wings (Konoha Tengu) or bird-like with human bodies but with birds' heads and strong beaks (Karasu Tengu); they play practical jokes on humans but may also help them and their king is Sōjōbō, depicted as an old bearded Tengu wearing the tiny hat of a Yama-bushi. Another curious creature is the Shōjō (said to be derived from the Orang-Utan of the Malay Archipelago) who is shown as a kind of monkey with a human face and long red hair, from which a dye is said to be made. It is caught by using a bait of *sake*, for which it has a craving.

Several legends and semi-historical romances form the subjects of Nō plays and as such occur on many objects. Typical of this class of subject is the representation of Jō and Uba, the spirits of the pine trees at Takasago and Suminoe, who appear as an old man with a rake and an old woman with a broom: they are symbols of longevity and happy old age. Another legend in this group is that of the life of Ono no Komachi, a ninth-century poetess. A common series of themes in art is that of the Shichi Komachi (Seven Komachi)—seven famous incidents in her life. She is one of the Rokkasen or Six Great Poets of the ninth century. Another poetess, Murasaki

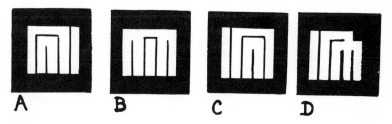

Examples of *Genji-Mon*. These devices, often found on color prints and some-times on *netsuke*, are each associated with a chapter of the tenth-century romance, the *Genji-monogatari* by Murasaki Shikibu, e.g. *A*. Chap. 46. *B*. Chap. 49. *C*. Chap. 43. *D*. Chap. 11. However, on lacquer and elsewhere some may function as true Mons, e.g. *D*. is also the Mon of Satake, Daimyō of Akita in Dewa.

Shikibu, is quite often shown sitting in the temple of Ishiyamadera in the moonlight, looking out over Lake Biwa and composing the famous romance *Genji-monogatari*, which itself provides many incidents as subject matter of art. Also found are the curious devices called *Genjimon*, each of which is a kind of monogram or cipher denoting one of the chapters of the book. This is a small sample of the vast and, indeed, almost limitless realm of fact and fancy, myth and legend, history and folklore, which may provide the subject matter for any decorative design.

Festivals, dances and pilgrimages

Aspects of these are all very frequently represented on Japanese *objets d'art* made during the Edo period and are therefore very likely to be met with by collectors. Of festivals (*matsuri*), one of the most important is that of the New Year (*shinnen*). On New Year's Eve black beans (*kuro mame*) were scattered to the four quarters in the house with the accompanying cry "Oni wa sato; fuka wa uchi" ("Clear out, devils; good luck to this house"). Gateways were then decorated with a sort of truss of pine and bamboo (*kado-matsu*)— sometimes seen on lacquer and sword guards—and strung across them was the *shimenawa*, a left-hand twisted rice-straw rope. This last is very frequently seen on art objects of all kinds, not only in this connection but binding together the Husband and Wife Rocks (*Mioto no seki*) at Futami-ga-ura, linking old Cryptomerias in temple groves, stretched across highways to keep off illness from a community, hung outside the forges of swordsmiths and, in February and October, hung between the summit of the cliff and a pine tree below, at Kinomoto where Izanagi is supposed to be buried. To the New Year *shimenawa* are attached a crayfish, a fern, leaves of *yuzuri* (*Daphniphyllum macropodum*), a plant indicative of successive generations, seaweed and the paper *gohei*. *Mochi* (round rice cakes) are made and games like *Oibane-kobane* (battledore and shuttlecock) are played. Groups of the *eta* class—a proscribed caste—performed the Lion Dance (*Shishimai*) in the streets, a man in a "lion" (*shishi*) mask prancing around to the rhythm of a drum. *Setsubun*, a movable feast at which beans were scattered, came in January or February.

Hina-matsuri (Doll's festival) was the girls' feast, when dolls representing the court were set out and sweet rice wine offered to them. *Tango-no-sekku* or Boys' Festival, held on the fifth day of the fifth month, was marked by the gift of a wooden sword, miniature armor, etc., and an inflatable kite in the form of a carp was flown; an iris (*ayame*) was dedicated to this day. Chrysanthemum viewing took place at the Feast of Happiness (*Chōyō-no-setsu*) on the ninth day of the ninth month. Moon viewing (*tsuki mi*) was held at the August full moon. A procession of decorated festival cars (*hoko*) with a Beauty Queen, dancers and musicians marked the Sannō *matsuri* on the fifteenth day of the seventh month and a similar festival, the *Gion*, was held in Kyōto: both figure frequently in art. *Niwaka* was a festival of the Yoshiwara with all the grades of courtesans (*oiran, shinzō* and *kamura*), geisha and the jesters (*hōkan*) and can usually be identified by the cars (*nerimono*) with scenery on them and by the convolvulus-shaped lanterns which are hung out. Many of these are still celebrated.

Dances, so often shown either as such or by the depicting of one or other of the items of associated paraphernalia, are classified into two kinds, the *mai*, which are ancient, and the *odori*, which are modern and popular. Among those usually found in art are: the *chō-odori*, in which the dancers have butterfly wings on their shoulders; the *sambasō* dance in which the chief performer wears the old man mask (*okina*) with hairy tufts on the forehead and carries a fan; the *Shakkyō*, or lion dance, in which the dancer is clothed in long red hair and carries peonies, and the *Shishimai*, another lion dance.

The above only touches on the extremely vast range of subjects that are to be found on art objects. In the Edo period, and even before, there was a large number of books, prints and paintings which were frankly erotic in intention and subject, some of which were also serious works of art; many more were only erotic by implication, and this was also true of some *netsuke*. Others, which sometimes appear erotic to Westerners, such as Kintoki or Kintarō (the golden boy) and Yama Uba (the old woman of the mountain) really Yaegiri, his mother, are in fact not so.

Further Reading

Joly, H. L., *Legend in Japanese Art*, London, 1907. (A most useful but very expensive single volume work but with several inaccuracies.)

Allen, M. R., *Japanese Art Motives*, Chicago, 1917. (A very useful and little-known work.)

Stewart, B., *Subjects Portrayed in Japanese Colour Prints*, London, 1922.

Ryerson, E., (*see under* Netsuke).

Edmunds, W. H., *Pointers and Clues to the Subjects of Chinese and Japanese Art*, London, 1934. (Possibly the most reliable of all such works.)

Weber, M. V. F., *Kōji Hōten*, 2 vols., Paris, 1923. (Most extensive of all, but contains many errors. A corrected edition is much desired.)

Binyon, L., *Catalogue of Japanese and Chinese Prints in the British Museum*, London, 1916.

Anderson, W., *Descriptive and Historical Catalogue of a Collection of Japanese and Chinese Paintings in the British Museum*, London, 1886. (Still useful.)

Toki, H., "Si-do-in-dzou. Gestes de l'officiant dans les ceremonies mystiques des sectes Tendai et Singon', trad. S. Kawamoura, Paris, *Ann. du Musee Guimet Bibliotheque d'études*, vol. viii, 1889. (Still useful for the mudras of images used in esoteric Buddhism. *See under* Buddhism, esp. Saunders.)

Ball, K. M., *Decorative Motives of Oriental Art*, London, 1927. (An excellent work.)

Hawley, F., *Art Symbols*, Oriental Culture Charts No. 12, Hollywood, n.d.

Appendices

I

A SHORT GUIDE TO THE MODERN
VALUES OF JAPANESE WORKS OF ART

ALMOST all Japanese art is selling for increasing prices month by month and it is fairly obvious that we are entering one of the phases of increased enthusiasm shown by collectors for this art in fairly regularly recurring cycles of approximately twenty years. Each time this has occurred prices have risen higher, not only because money has depreciated, but also because more works of art have gone out of circulation into museums, more have returned to Japan itself, and a few more have suffered destruction and decay. Moreover, with the exception of a very short period after the Second World War when some very old, rare and highly important works of art left the country—mostly destined for the major museums of the U.S.A.—the export of all major works of art has been forbidden by the Japanese Government. Even so, price variations and increases are uneven and although *netsuke* prices are rising rapidly to un-imagined peaks, paintings remain procurable, if but rarely, for more moderate figures, e.g. a fine scroll by Tani Bunchō was offered by a British dealer for $56 in 1961.

Some lacquer remains reasonable: a gold lacquer display cabinet of the type coming to Europe in the seventeenth century brought $20 (Sotheby, 1961); a fine five-case Shibayama *Inrō* (early) $45 (Sotheby, 1961); two fine *Inrō* from the Tomkinson collection—one with pottery inlay of shells, $56 the two (Sotheby, 1961); a fine *Bunko* case in *kinji* lacquer with autumn flowers and interior tray with *nade-shiko* $140 (Sotheby, 1961); a pair of extremely fine Shibayama screens signed Shikakusai Shibafune, $1,120; indeed, fine *inrō* may fetch in good sales anything from $28 to $500 and this difference seems often more dependent on the subject than on the style or age. Rarely, good quality *inrō* can be found in the provinces still for around $15. Pouches (*kinchaku*, etc.) with first-class *Kanamono* in ivory or metal may bring $30 to $90, but very good second-class specimens are to be obtained for much less. Fine bronze vases of fairly recent date have fetched surprisingly high prices, e.g. an exceptional one in the style of Natsuo reached $106 (Sotheby, 1961). Mostly, however, bronzes are still relatively cheap and some very charming small animal bronzes become available from time to time for $10 to $25. Although still scorned for the most part by the more "highbrow" of *netsuke* collectors, ivory Okimono are rising in price, few going for less than $25 each for good-quality carvings and very exceptional ones have reached $200 and much more. *Netsuke* are most variable: fine eighteenth-century wood *netsuke* can still be bought for under $25 each, even when of the finest quality, although for rare subjects, signed pieces by famous carvers and such, one may have to pay up to $90, but this is unusual. Ivory *netsuke*, on the other hand, are generally more expensive and few that are lotted singly in the great London salesrooms will go for under $20 and really outstanding and exceptional ones have fetched $460: nevertheless, groups of good *netsuke* sometimes go for much less, e.g. a nice lot of six with two signed Tomochika and Mitsuyuki respectively went for $56 to a great London dealer in oriental art. However, the beginner must be warned that there are many poor ivory specimens, roughly carved and quite undesirable, that he will be offered for $2 or $3 and which he will be well advised to leave so that they may give pleasure to someone likely to remain unsophisticated in these things.

Swords and sword furniture are still among the more moderately priced forms of art. A truly outstanding *Tantō* blade, of superb quality in all respects, with the scabbard, signed "Sanseisai Yokei" reached only $224 (Sotheby, 1961). Quite desirable mounted swords, especially if in a lot of two or three with one of them damaged may average about $15 a piece and a most interesting collection of *kozuka* handles in the same sale as above, twenty-four pieces in all, went for $106, and one can only think they must increase in value. Quite respectable iron *tsuba* may sometimes go for little more than $3 each, but usually one is forced to pay two or three times this. Detailed work on any *tsuba* will enhance the prices enormously and probably those in *shakudō* are in the greatest demand and may well bring above $90 each, particularly if they show fish or insects or some similar subject, but the collector will find many others available and some well worth obtaining at under $15. *Fuchikashira* of really fine quality and very desirable often go for under $5. *Menuki* may attain rather higher prices and really fine ones such as those of the Gotō school may bring much more. Articulated iron animal models of really fine quality usually sell for between $80 and $225 each, but are seldom offered. Other arms of equal quality and not of such interest to collectors usually fetch correspondingly smaller prices. In the last five or six years at Glendining's sales, a fine *naginata* sold for $21 and a good suit of *tatami-dō* armor with the mon of Hondo no Masatada for $27. Of arrowheads, $15 or so will buy a very good one and they can be obtained for less, but a fine example of a Japanese eighteenth-century matchlock gun brought $140 at Sotheby's. Of cloisonné work one can only say there is as yet little stability in the prices, but $30 to $40 should buy a very fair example of late nineteenth-century work. Bamboo work and *hyōtan* appear from time to time in mixed lots with almost anything else from broken bracelets to Babylonian clay tablets—the collector must watch his opportunity.

Fine textiles are rarely offered for sale in England and seem more common in French sales. Embroidered wall panels of small size and nineteenth-century date are most frequent and generally command something under $20. Fine *kimono* of nineteenth-century date may bring up to $60 and good specimens of *yuzen* work will bring more. *Nō* robes have always fetched large prices if genuine and good and will no doubt continue to demand sums of three or even four figures. Prices of ceramics, still relatively cheap, continue to rise: an Arita porcelain plaque bought in 1954 for $12 fetched $35 in 1961 and, although this is perhaps exceptional, there is little doubt that prices of six or seven years ago have at least doubled. Late Satsuma ware still has its followers to the extent of some $30 or so for a pair of not too ornate vases; this is surprising. There are surprises here in other prices: a lot of six nice teapots including one in Ise-Banko ware and another signed "Shuzan" fetched only $15 at Glendining's in 1956. Respectable tea bowls may still be bought for under $70;

from the smaller dealer and by the vigilant collector sometimes for under $60.

With prints much depends on condition, rarity and (all eighteenth-century prints are distinctly rarer than they were thirty years ago) and aesthetic appeal. Top prices for those that combine all three are perhaps the best guide; Hiroshige's great triptych *The Rapids of Awa no Naruto*, a superb impression, $300 (Glendining's); Sharaku's portrait of Sawamura Sōjuro III, slightly rubbed and stained, $475 (Glendining's, 1961); Harunobu, *hashirakake* of an *oiran* (slight repair and soiling) $95; a Harunobu *chuban* in almost perfect condition $770. A fair "Primitive" sheet costs today $30 to $90 and a really fine Utamaro, Kōryusai or Kiyonaga may range more widely from $25 to $250; but without rarity, interesting single sheet Hiroshige prints can be obtained for $6 to $15 upwards and such as Sugakudo's bird and flower prints for an average of $6 upwards.

II

A SHORT BIBLIOGRAPHY OF
GENERAL WORKS ON JAPANESE ART

Swann, P. C., *An Introduction to the Arts of Japan*, Oxford, 1958. (Quite the best English history of Japanese art. The historical approach is carried out through the whole book, all the arts are dealt with and finely illustrated.)

Buhot, J., *Histoire des Arts du Japon*, Paris, 1949. (A fine and scholarly work but only one volume has yet appeared and that is very expensive.)

Paine, R. T., and Soper, A., *The Art and Architecture of Japan*, London, 1955. (Completely authoritative, well illustrated, but deals only with painting, sculpture and architecture.)

Munsterberg, H., *The Arts of Japan*, 1957.

Tōkyō National Museum Staff, *Pageant of Japanese Art*, 6 vols., Tōkyō, 1952–60. (A most important work with much that is new and adequately illustrated in the small edition which is nevertheless much cheaper.)

Minamoto, H., *An Illustrated History of Japanese Art*. (Important, especially for the earlier art, and very finely illustrated.)

Tsuda, N., *Handbook of Japanese Art*, Tōkyō, 1935. (A most useful guide.)

Yoneyama and Wakai, *Kokuho Mokuroku*, Nara, 1925. (A catalogue of National Treasure which any unguided student of serious intention in Japan must consult.)

Fenollosa, E., *Epochs of Chinese and Japanese Art*, New York, 1921. (Still of value although the author's treatment of the eighteenth and nineteenth centuries is not considered to be valid today.)

Bing, M. S., *Collection Barboutau*, 2 vols., Paris, 1904. (An immense and luxurious sale catalogue covering all the arts with full descriptions and most important explanatory notes and biographies.)

Tajima, S., *Selected Relics of Japanese Art*, 20 vols., Tōkyō, 1899–1908. (Text in Japanese and English. The most comprehensive illustrated source book.)

Kokusai Bunka Shinkokai, *Bibliography of reference books for Japanese studies*, vol. 7, Arts and Crafts, Tōkyō, 1959.

III

A SHORT NOTE ON THE
READING OF INSCRIPTIONS

THE madly enthusiastic student will try to learn a little written Japanese—quite different from that which is spoken—this will not lessen his enthusiasm, but will probably break his heart; it is the world's most difficult written language. One less enthusiastic will at least wish to read signatures and for this he must before long possess Koop and Inada's *Japanese Names and How to Read Them*, London, 1923 (new ed. printing). To use this great book is, inevitably, nearly as difficult as learning Japanese, but in it is the student's only hope; he must have it and he must try. But which is the signature? Look for such words as *saku* (1), *sei* (2), *zō* (3), all of which may also be read *tsukuru* and all of which mean "made" (=fecit). Sometimes this is followed by *kore* (4) meaning "this" which is read before the verb, e.g. *Kore* (*wo*) *tsukuru*, i.e. "made this." Other verbs to look for are *gwa* (5), *no hitsu* (6), *no dzu* (7), all of which mean "painted" or "drew," or *no tō* (8) "carved," or *sho* (9) "wrote," or *chō* (10) *koku* (11) or *sen* (12) which mean "chased" or "engraved"; anything from two to five or six characters in front of these, reading downwards, will be the name you are looking for. Very rarely there may be only one character. For dates, look for any of the numerals interspersed with such characters as *nen* (13) "year," or *tsuki* (14) "month," or *nichi* (15) "day"; by themselves these may give the year, etc., of the sexagenary cycle if combined with the *junishi* and *jikkan* (*see* under) or of the *nengō* (reign title), and should be read as such.

作 1. 製 2. 造 3. 之 4. 畫 5.

筆 6. 圖 7. 刀 8. 書 9. 彫 10.

刻 11. 鐫 12. 年 13. 月 14. 日 15.

NUMERALS

1	一	壹	ICHI	HITO †
2	二	貳	NI	FUTA
3	三	参	SAN	MI
4	四	肆	SHI	YO
5	五	伍	GŌ	ITSU
6	六	陸	RŌKU	MU
7	七	柒	SHICHI	NANA
8	八	捌	HACHI	YA
9	九	玖	KU	KONONO
10	十	拾	JU	TŌ
15	十五		JUGŌ	
20	二十		NIJU	

First column gives arabic numeral.

Second column Japanese numeral.

Third column the full form in Japanese sometimes used for ornamental purposes on works of art.

Fourth column the sinico-Japanese reading.

Fifth column the pure Japanese reading.

(Both the latter may occur in names.)

† This character very frequently occurs in names and may be read Ichi, Itsu, Kazu, Hito, hitotsu or I. In the last instance, before the consonants 's', 'k' and 'p' when they commence the next syllable of the name, they are doubled; thus, not 'Ishiki' but 'Isshiki'.

Common Seal Forms. 𠂊 𠃌 寅 卯 辰 巳 午 未 申 酉 戌 亥

NE USHI TORA U TATSU MI UMA HITSUJI SARU TORI INU I

		子	丑	寅	卯	辰	巳	午	未	申	酉	戌	亥
Ki no e	甲	1		51		41		31		21		11	
Ki no to	乙		2		52		42		32		22		12
Hi no e	丙	13		3		53		43		33		23	
Hi no to	丁		14		4		54		44		34		24
Tsuchi no e	戊	25		15		5		55		45		35	
Tsuchi no to	己		26		16		6		56		46		36
Ka no e	庚	37		27		17		7		57		47	
Ka no to	辛		38		28		18		8		58		48
Mizu no e	壬	49		39		29		19		9		59	
Mizu no to	癸		50		40		30		20		10		60

In dates the year is sometimes given by indicating its order in the sixty years (sexagenary) cycle which was probably in use from A.D. 424. Recent cycles began in 1864, 1804, 1744, 1684, 1624, 1564, 1504, 1444, 1384 and 1324, etc. For this purpose the Ten 'Stems' are combined with the Twelve 'Branches' in the manner given in the above table. The twelve 'Branches' (*Junishi*) are sometimes given alone and the year is then known by the name of the zodiacal animal to which each 'Branch' refers. These are in order: Rat, Ox, Tiger, Hare, Dragon, Snake, Horse, Goat, Ape, Cock, Dog and Hog. These cycles of twelve may be worked out from the years given above, each of these being the year of the Rat. On color prints and more rarely on some other things, the *Junishi* are given in their seal form and for some years these were combined with the official 'aratame' and 'kiwame' seals of the censors. (See under color prints.) The numeral, often combined in the same seal refers to the month of the year in which the print was issued.

寬正 KWANSHŌ 1460	文正 BUNSHŌ 1466	應仁 Ō-NIN 1467	文明 BUMMEI 1469	長享 CHŌKŌ 1487	延德 ENTOKU 1489	明應 MEI-Ō 1492	文龜 BUNKI 1501	永正 EISHŌ 1504
大永 PAI-EI 1521	享祿 KOROKU 1528	天文 TEMBUN 1532	弘治 KŌJI 1555	永祿 EIROKU 1558	元龜 GENKI 1570	天正 TENSHŌ 1573	文祿 BUNROKU 1592	慶長 KEICHŌ 1596
元和 GENWA 1615	寬永 KWANEI 1624	正保 SHŌHŌ 1644	慶安 KEIAN 1648	承應 JŌ-Ō 1652	明曆 MEIREKI 1655	萬治 MANJI 1658	寬文 KWAMBUN 1661	延寶 EMPŌ 1673
天和 TENWA 1681	貞享 JŌKŌ 1684	元祿 GENROKU 1688	寶永 HŌEI 1704	正德 SHŌTOKU 1711	享保 KŌHŌ 1716	元文 GEMBUN 1736	寬保 KWAMPŌ 1741	延享 ENKŌ 1744
寬延 KWANEN 1748	寶曆 HŌREKI 1751	明和 MEIWA 1764	安永 ANEI 1772	天明 TEMMEI 1781	寬政 KWANSEI 1789	享和 KŌWA 1801	文化 BUNKWA 1804	文政 BUNSEI 1818
天保 TEMPŌ 1830	弘化 KŌKWA 1844	嘉永 KAEI 1848	安政 ANSEI 1854	萬延 MAN-EN 1860	文久 BUNKYU 1861	元治 GENJI 1864	慶應 KEI-Ō 1865	明治 MEIJI 1868

Table of Nengō. The Nengō are names of good augury given to periods of years which in Japan, unlike China, do not, or but rarely, correspond with the reigns of the emperors. They are often used in dating works of art and the above table gives the characters, readings and years in which they commenced.

TABLES OF CHARACTERS USED IN NAMES

	1	2	3	4	5	6	7	8	9	10	11	12	13
A	家	一	春	治	玄	張	晴	秦	日	入	仁	崔	堀
B	友	倫	朝	具	知	共	顆	朋	侖	住	才	利	俊
C	咸	年	壽	時	李	豐	當	遠	虎	同	近	親	周
D	丁	刀	立	馬	文	珍	調	袋	川	羽	斐	北	居
E	湖	力	興	音	乀	往	兼	包	勝	旲	晩	皇	和
F	方	上	吉	溪	木	湖	麿	倍	義	善	能	良	賀
G	賢	度	克	祥	如	覽	賴	依	仍	白	歸	馮	夜
H	忠	豆	智	俎	當	焉	高	貴	李	安	宣	尾	奧

The 312 characters given here are those most frequently occurring in the names of various groups of artists and craftsmen, determined by a frequency count. It is a well-known but puzzling fact among collectors that Japanese characters, almost without exception, have several possible readings and apart from the difficulty experienced in finding the character in a dictionary this multiplicity of readings causes further bewilderment. It is hoped that the presentation adopted here will make the matter a little easier and give the collector the means of reading some six or seven of every ten names which he finds in signatures. For those in highly cursive script he will need a dictionary of *Sōsho* forms such as that of O. Daniells.

Readings of the characters given here are those mostly to be found in use and, as a further guide the kind of artist frequently using any reading is indicated in brackets. These are: (*m*) metalworkers including armorers and swordsmiths; (*p*) print artists, i.e. ukiyo-e designers; (*pa*) painters; (*l*) lacquers workers; (*pot*) potters and (*n*) netsuke carvers. Naturally, any one reading may be used by all these groups without being so designated. N.B. Most pure Japanese readings are of two syllables and are never mixed with sinico-Japanese readings, e.g. Toshitomo NOT Toshirin.

A.
1. Iye (*m*), Ka, Ke, He, Ye.
2. Ichi, itsu (*p*), kazu.
3. Haru (*m,p*), shun (*pa*).
4. Haru, chi, Ji.
5. Haru, Gen (*n*)
6. Haru, Chō, Hari.
7. Haru, Sei, Shō
8. Hata (*m*), Shin, Jin.
9. Nichi, Hi.
10. Nyu, Iri, Iru.
11. Ni, Jin, Nin, Hito.
12. Koku (*m*), Goku, Tobu.
13. Hori (*m*), Kutsu, Kuchi.

B.
1. Tomo, Yu.
2. Tomo, Sane, Rin, Muni.
3. Tomo, Chō, Asa.
4. Tomo (*m*), Ku, Gu.
5. Tomo, Chika, Aki, Chi, Shi.
6. Tomo, Maga, Kiō, Gu.
7. Tomo (*m*).
8. Tomo, Hō.
9. Tomo, Rin.
10. Tomo, Chu, Ju, Sumi.
11. Sai, Zai.
12. Toshi, Ri, To.
13. Toshi (*m*), Shun (*p*).

C.
1. Toshi, Sei, Aai.
2. Toshi, Nen, Ne.
3. Toshi (*m*), Naga, Hisa, Ju, Su, Zu.
4. Toki, Ji (Shi).
5. Toki (*m*), Toshi, Ki, Suye.
6. Toyo (*m*), (*p*), Hō, Bu, Fu.
7. Tomi (*m*), Fu, Ton, To.
8. Tō (*m*), Yen, On, O.
9. Tora, Ko, Ku.
10. Dō (*m*), Kane, Atsu, Nobu, Ai.
11. Chika.
12. Chika (*n*), Shin.
13. Chika, Kane, Shu, Su.

D.
1. Ryo (*m*), Masa.
2. Riki, Rioku.
3. Ryu (*m*), Ritsu, Tatsu, Tate (*pa*).
4. Ba (*p, n*), Uma, -ma.
5. Bun (*p, n*), Mon, Mo, Fumi, Bumi.
6. Chin (*p*), Yoshi, Udzu, Taka, Nori.
7. Chō, Ju, Tsuki.
8. Tai, Tei, Fukuro.
9. Gawa (Kawa) (*p*).
10. Hane (*p*), U, Ha, -wa.
11. Hishi, Rishi.
12. Hoku, Kita (*p*).
13. I (*p*), Kio, Ko, Yasu, Yori.

E.
1. Chō (*p*), Shio, Ushio.
2. Ishi (*p, pa*), Seki (*pa*), Jaku, Koku Iwa.
3. Oki (*p*), Kiō, Kō.
4. Oto (*p*) (*pot*), Ne, In, On.
5. Oto (*m*), Itsu, -otsu.
6. O (*m*), Wa.
7. Kane—several varieties of this character.
8. Kane (*m*), Hō.
9. Katsu (*m*) (*p*), Shō.
10. Kage (*m*), Kei (*pa*), Kiō.
11. Kage, Ban, Man.
12. Kazu (*m*), Riō.
13. Kazu, Wa, Kwa.

F.
1. Kata, Hō, Ha, Michi, Masa, Fusa.
2. Kami, Jō, Kō, Shō, Uye.
3. Yoshi (*m*), Kichi, Ki.
4. Kei (*p*), Tani, Ke.
5. Ki (*p, pot*), (*l*), Shige, Moku, Boku, Kō.
6. Ko (*p*), Umi.
7. Maro.
8. Masu (*p*), Be, Hai, Bai.
9. Yoshi (*m*), Gi.
10. Yoshi (*m*), Sen, Zen (*p*).
11. Yoshi (*m*), Do, No (*l*) (*pa*).
12. Yori (*m*), Rio, Ra, Naga, Haru.
13. Yoshi (*m*), Ka (*pot*), Ga.

G.
1. Yoshi, Ken, Kata.
2. Yoshi, Dzu, To, Tabi.
3. Yoshi (*m*), Katsu, Nari, Koku.
4. Yoshi (*m*), Shon (*pot*), Shō, Sō.
5. Yoshi (*m*), Yuki, Nio, Jo.
6. Yoshi (*m*), Kaku, Sato, Ko.
7. Yori (*m*), Rai.
8. Yori (*m*), Yo (*pa*), Ye.
9. Yori, Jō, Niō.
10. Yori (*m*), Kore, Ji, Tada.
11. Yori (*m*), Kayeri (*pa*), Moto, Ki.
12. Yori, Hio, Bio.
13. Yoru (*m*), Ya, Yo, Yasu.

H.
1. Tada, Chu.
2. Tada, Sen.
3. Tomo (*m*), Toshi, Chi.
4. Tada, So, Zo, Yuku.
5. Tō (*m*), Ta, Taye, Masu.
6. Tame (*m*), I (*p*).
7. Take, Ko.
8. Take, Ki.
9. Taka (*m*), Yoshi, Nari, Kō, Kio.
10. Yasu (*m, pa*), An (*pa*), A (*pa*).
11. Nobu (*p*), Nori, Sen.
12. O (*p*), Bi, Mi.
13. Oku (*p*), O.

	I	J	K	L	M	N	O	P
13	經	斗	宗	順	延	匡	伏	明
12	恒[A]	翼	南	德	信	當	不[A]	鑑[A]
11	綱	標	奈	俵	度	昌	風[A]	觀
10	續	鉛	波	辟	意	改	藤	題[A]
9	次	飾	中	數	應	正	冬	秋
8	龍	之	仲	法	芳	補	英	在
7	造	篤	業	則	美	保	房	有
6	種	局	成	瓜	榮	泰	松[A]	小
5	竹	藤	尚	石	歌	唐	乃[A]	伊
4	武	朗	直[A]	梅	烏	月	又	惟
3	呂	理	長	雲	給	軍	丸[A]	是
2	隆[A]	樂	水	村	氏	國	布[A]	佛
1	育[A]	常	貴	吉[A]	憲	實	增	二

i.

1. Iku, Yoku.
2. Taka, Riu.
3. Miya, Taka, Kiu, Ku-, Gu-.
4. Take (*m*), Bu, Mu.
5. Take (*m*), Chiku (*n*).
6. Tane (*m*), Shô, Shu, -kusa (fusa, kazu).
7. Michi, Ki, Gi.
8. Tatsu (*m*), riu (*p*), riô.
9. Tsugu (*m*), Shi, Ji, Su, Tsugi-.
10. Tsugu (*m*), Shoku, Zoku, tsugi-.
11. Tsuna (*m*), Kô.
12. Tsune (*m*), Kô, Gô.
13. Tsune (*m*), Kei, Kiô, Fu, He (yoshi).

j.

1. Tsune (*m*), Jo (*l*), Shô, To.
2. Raku (*p*), -Ra.
3. Ri (*p*), Osamu (tadá, masa).
4. Rô (*p*), Sei, Shi, Se, nari.
5. Sai (*p*), Sei, Shi, Se, nari.
6. Sen (*p*), ôgi.
7. Sha (*p*), also to be read 'utsusu', i.e. to copy.
8. Shi (*p*), No, Yuki.
9. Shika (*p*), Shoku).
10. Suyu (*p*), Rei, Riô.
11. Tachihana (*p*),
12. Tai (*p*),
13. To (*p*), Tô, Tsu (maru).

k.

1. Tsura (*m*), Nuki, Kwan.
2. Naga (*pot*) (*l*) (*m*), Yei, Yô.
3. Naga (*m*), Chô (*l*).
4. Nao (*m*), Choku, Jiki.
5. Nao (*m*), Shô, Jô, Hisa.
6. Nari (*m*), Sei, Jô, Naru, Shige.
7. Nari (*m*), Giô, Gô, Waza.
8. Naka (*m*), Chu.
9. Naka (*m, pot., pa., l*), Chu (*pa*).
10. Nami (*m*), Ha, Dai.
11. Na (*m*), Dai, Nai.
12. Nan (*m*), Na, Minami, Mina.
13. Mune (*m*), Sô (*l*).

L.

1. Mune (*m*), Shi.
2. Mura (*m, p*).
3. Un (*m*), U. Kumo.
4. Ume (*m*), Bai, Mai.
5. Iwa, ishi (*pa, pot*), Seki (*pa*), Jaku Koku, Ha.
6. Uri (*m*), Kwa, Ke.
7. Nori (*m*), Soku, So.
8. Nori, Hô (*m*), Fu.
9. Nori (*m*), Kô, Kiô.
10. Kan, Kara.
11. Nori (*m*), Gi, Yoshi.
12. Nori (*m*), Toku, To, Tsuku.
13. Nori (*m*), Jun, Shun, Yasu, Nobu, Masa, Yuki, Toshi, Yori, Yoshi, Mune.

M.

1. Nori (*m*), Ken, Kon, teru.
2. Uji (*m*), Shi, Ji.
3. Yu, Yutaka, Yasu, Hiro.
4. Tori (*p, pa*), Chô, To (*pa*).
5. Uta (*p*), Ka.
6. Yei (*p*), Yô, Hisa, Teru, Shige, Naga, Yoshi, Haru, Saka, Hide.
7. Yoshi (*p, l*), Bi, Mi, Haru, Tomi.
8. Yoshi (*p*), Hô, Ha (*pa*).
9. Nori (*m*), Yô, O, Yoshi, Mune, Oki.
10. Nori (*m*), I, O, Moto, Mune, Oki.
11. Nori (*m*), To, Dzu, Do, tabi.
12. Nobu (*m, p*), Shin, Shi.
13. Nobu (*m*), Yen, Ye, Nobe.

N.

1. Nobu (*m*), Sen, Nori.
2. Kuni, Koku, Ku.
3. Gun (*m*).
4. Gwatsu, Getsu, Tsuki.
5. Tô, Dô, Kara.
6. Yasu (*m*), Tai (*l*).
7. Yasu (*m*), Hô, O.
8. Yasu, Hô, Fu, Sada.
9. Masa (*m*), Shô (*l*).
10. Masa (*m, p*), Sei, Shô.
11. Masa, Shô (*p*).
12. Masa, Tô, ta, -taye.
13. Masa, Kiô, Kô.

o.

1. Masu, So, Zo, Mashi.
2. Mare (*m*), Ki, Ke.
3. Maru (*m*), Kwan, Gwan, Wei
4. Mata (*m*), Yu, U.
5. Man (*m*), Ban.
6. Matsu (*m*), Shô.
7. Fusa (*m*), Hô, Bô.
8. Fusa (*m*), Yei (*p*), Yô, Hide, Teru.
9. Fuyu (*m*), Tô.
10. Fuji (*m*), Tô, Dô.
11. Fu, Fuji (*pot*), Kaza, Kaze.
12. Fu.
13. Fushi (*m*), Fuku, Buku, Fuse.

p.

1. Futa (*m*), Ni, Ji.
2. Butsu (*m*), Futsu.
3. Kore (*m*), Shi, Ji, Ze, (Yoshi, Yuke).
4. Kore (*m*), I, Tada, Nobu.
5. Kore (*m*), I, Tada.
6. Kô (*m*), Shô, O.
7. Ari (*m*), Yu, U, Zai.
8. Ari (*m*), Zai.
9. Aki (*m*), Shu, Ai.
10. Aki (*m*), Ken, Gen.
11. Aki (*m*), Kwan (mi, chika)
12. Aki (*m*), Kan, Ken, (nori, kane).
13. Aki (*m*), Mei, Mio, Min, Ake.

	Q	R	S	T	U	V	W	X
13	山	雫	水	氏	用	季	玉	朝
12	西	幸	十	平	持	末	人	祐
11	左	行	心	衡	師	普	郎	鸞
10	寶	喜	新	秀	本	相	窩	加
9	眞	嚳	丁	久	基	佐	園	亮
8	定	金	戈	禮	元	員	亭	猿
7	貝	神	鎭	嚴	夏	祐	舎	愛
6	淡	氷	重	野	林	伞	軒	俠
5	天	浪	通	門	森	助	堂	古
4	鵈	干	道	寛	守	仙	甬	彌
3	敦	清	三	弘	盛	泉	牧	出
2	銘	口	滿	廣	彦	千	住	阿
1	章	散	光	四	七	百	純	梶

Q.
1. Aki (m), Shō (p), Sō.
2. Aki (m), Mei, Miō.
3. Atsu (m), Ton, Shun, Jun.
4. Atsu (m, p), Toku.
5. Ama (m), Ten, Te, Ame.
6. Awa (m), Tan, Dan.
7. Sada (m, p), Tei, Jō.
8. Sada, Tei, Jō.
9. Sane (m), Shin, Ma.
10. Sane (m), Jitsu, Jichi.
11. Sa (suke).
12. Sai (m), Nishi (p), Sei.
13. San (m), Sen (p), Yama, -Zan.

R.
1. San, Sa.
2. Kuchi, - guchi.
3. Kiyo (m), Sei, Shō, Shin.
4. Ne, Tsu, Shi, Ko.
5. Kiyo (m), Rō, Ra, Nami, Na.
6. Kiyo (m), Hiō, Hii.
7. Kiyo (m), Ko, Shin, Jin, Mi, Kani, Kan.
8. Kin (m), Kon, Kane, Kana.
9. Kiku (m), Koku.
10. Ki (m), Yoshi (p).
11. Yuki, Kō, Giō, An.
12. Yuki (m), Kō.
13. Yuki, Setsu, Sechi.

S.
1. Mitsu, Kō (n).
2. Mitsu (m, p), Ma (l), Ban, Man, -mero.
3. Mitsu, Mi, San, Sa.
4. Michi (m), Tō, Dō, Ji.
5. Michi, Tō, Rsu.
6. Shige (m, p), Chō, Ju, Ye.
7. Shige, Chin (Yasu).
8. Shige (m), Bō, Mo.
9. Shimo, Shita.
10. Shin (m), Shi, Ara, Nii.

11. Shin (m), Sane, Kiyo, Mune.
12. Ju (m), Shu, So, To, Jitsu-, Jutsu-.
13. Midzu, Sui, Mi.

τ. 1. Shi (m), Yo, Yotsu.
2. Hiro (m, p), Ko, Kwō.
3. Hiro (m, l), Kō, Ga.
4. Hiro (m), Kwan.
5. Hiro (m), Mon.
6. Hiro (m), No (l).
7. Hiro (m), Gen, Gon.
8. Hiro (m), Nori, Rei, Rai, Re.
9. Hisa (m), Kui, Ku (pot).
10. Hide (m, n), Shu, Su.
11. Hira (m), Kō, Giō.
12. Hira (m, pot, pa), Hei, Hiō, He.
13. Hiō, Hei.

u. 1. Shitsu, Shichi, Nana.
2. Hiko (m), Gen.
3. Mori (m), Sei, Jō.
4. Mori (m, p), Shu.
5. Mori (m), Shin.
6. Mori (m), Rin, Shige.
7. Mori (m), Yen.
8. Moto (m), Gen, Gwan.
9. Moto (m), Ki.
10. Moto (m), Hon, Ho, Ne.
11. Moro (m, p), Shi.
12. Mochi (m), Chi, Ji.
13. Mochi (m), Yo, Yu.

v. 1. Momo (m), Hiaku, Haku, Mo, Do, -ho, -o.
2. Sen, Chi.
3. Sen (m, p), idzumi (pa).
4. Sen.
5. Suke, Jo, So.
6. Ima, Kin, Kon.
7. Suke, Yu, U.

8. Suke, Shi.
9. Sa (m, pa), Suke.
10. Suke, Shō, Sō, Ai, O.
11. Suga, Kan, Ken, Suge.
12. Suye, Batsu, Matsu, Ma.
13. Suye, Ki.

w. 1. Sumi, Shun, Jun.
2. Sumi (pa), Chu, Ju.
3. Sita, Hō.
4. Sumi (pot), Kaka, Koku, Tsuno, Kado.
5. Dō, Tō, Ta.
6. Ken, Kon, Kan (roki).
7. Sha, noya, ya (sometimes with J. in front and then read noya).
8. Tei, Chō, Chin, Te.
9. Yen (where prefix is of two syllables then often read zono).
10. Kwa.
11. Rō (often preceded in names by a numeral).
12. Jin, Nin, Hito.
13. Gioku (n), Tama (l).

x. 1. Kaji (l), Bi, Mi.
2. A (with X.4 is read-ami).
3. Shutsu, Shuchi, Sui, Idzu, Ide, De (Deme (n)).
4. Mi, Bi, Ya, Rya.
5. Ko, Furu, Hisa.
6. Kō, Go, Shiri.
7. Ai, Yei, Ye, Naru, Hide, Nari, Hisa, Yoshi, Chika.
8. Yen, On, Sa, Saru, Mashi.
9. Riō, Suke (n), Aki.
10. Ka (m, pa, pot, l)
11. Ran.
12. Suke (p), Yu, U.
13. Asa (m, pa), Chō, Tomo.

N.B.—The letter 'A' in the bottom right-hand corner of a character square indicates that it is either an alternative or abbreviated form of another character also found in signatures. Readings in parentheses are much less common and usually 'Nanori' ones.

Glossary of words descriptive of art objects and decoration and not occurring in the text

For terms used in the text, see Index.

Ajiro. A mode of weaving split bamboo. A bamboo mat.
Ao-e. A print or painting in blue.
Aratame. A round seal on prints which means 'examined'. Used 1854 to 1857. After 1859 combined with the date in one seal.

Baku. A mythical tapir-like animal which eats bad dreams.
Basen. A saddle cloth.
Biwa. A four-stringed lute.

Chabentō. A portable chest for making tea.
Chōban. A print size $20\frac{1}{2} \times 7\frac{1}{2}$ inches.
Chōdo-kake. A rack for bows and arrows.
Chōshi. A vessel for pouring *sake*.
Chuban. A print size $10 \times 7\frac{1}{2}$ inches.
Chu-tanzaku. A print size $15 \times 5\frac{1}{4}$ inches.

Dōhachi. A sacred vessel.

Fusuma. Sliding partitions.

Geimyō. A professional name.
Go. A game like checkers.
Gō. The personal pseudonym of an artist.
Gyotai. Ornamental bag worn by nobles.

Hakama. Long, loose trousers.
Hashira-e or **Hashirakake-e.** A long narrow print made for hanging on a pillar.
Hasamibako. A lacquered box fixed on the end of a pole.
Hokai. A cylindrical box for carrying food.
Hosoban (syn. **Hoso-e**). Print size $13 \times 7\frac{1}{2}$ inches.
Hossu. A fly-switch carried by priests.

Ichimatsu-some. A popular check dress material invented by the actor Sanogawa Ichimatsu.

Inu-bariko. Figures of dogs held by children as amulets.

Ishi-zuri. A print made from an engraved stone.

Jumotsu. Precious things preserved as relics in families and temples.

Juzu. A rosary.

Kago. A litter for carrying people.

Kamuro. A young maid to a harlot.

Katsui. A garment woven with grass fibres.

Kawara. A tile.

Kesa. A scarf worn by Buddhist priests.

Kiri-e. Picture with a mica ground.

Kiwame. A round seal meaning 'approved' put on prints.

Koban. Print size $9 \times 6\frac{1}{2}$ inches.

Kōro. An incense burner.

Ko-yotsugiri. Print size $6\frac{3}{4} \times 4\frac{1}{2}$ inches.

Kuge. Title of a court noble.

Kurenai-e. A picture in red used as a charm against smallpox.

Mameban. Any print size smaller than $6\frac{3}{4} \times 4\frac{1}{2}$ inches.

Mokugyō. A gong used by priests and resembling a large ferret's bell.

Nengō. The name given to a period of years, e.g. Meiji.

Nerimono. Ornaments of wax imitating coral, ivory, etc.

Norimono. A palanquin.

Ōban. Print size $15 \times 10\frac{1}{2}$ inches.

Obi. A girdle, sash or waistband.

Oi. A box with legs, carried on the back.

Orikami. A certificate of authenticity given by an expert.

Ō-tanzaku. A print size 15×7 inches.

Rokkasen. The six celebrated poets of ancient literature.

Ryaku-reki. Abbreviated almanacs.

Ryōgake. A pair of square boxes carried on a pole.

Sakayuki. A *sake* cup.

Sekitai. A belt.

Shakujō. A staff with rings carried by priests.

Shimadi. A stand on which is placed an ornamental arrangement of pine, bamboo, plum, figurines, etc., at weddings.

Shinzō. A young courtesan.

Suikan. A robe of thin silk.

Sumō. A form of wrestling.

Tanzaku. A card, variously ornamental, on which verses are written.

Tate-e. A vertical picture composition.

Tengai. A canopy erected over Buddhist figures.

Toshidama. A conventional representation of a New Year's gift which resembles a ring.

Tsugi-ga-hana. Technique of sharpening outlines of yuzen fabric designs by painting in.

Tsuitate. A one-leaf screen.

Tsuzumi. A hand drum.

Usuri-e. A print in very thin color.

Yaki-e. A drawing burnt in material by hot metal.

Yamabushi. Wandering priests who practice divination.

Yanaiba. A wicker box with a cover.

Yoko-e. A picture with horizontal composition.

Yujō. A grade of courtesan.

Note: The names of other and rarer sizes of Japanese prints now in standard usage by cataloguers are to be found detailed and explained in Schraubstadter, C., *Care and Repair of Japanese Prints*, New York, 1948.

INDEX